APACHE DAYS

AND

TOMBSTONE NIGHTS

APACHE DAYS
AND
TOMBSTONE NIGHTS

John Clum's Autobiography, 1877-1887

Edited by
Neil B. Carmony

High-Lonesome Books
Silver City, New Mexico
1997

———————

ISBN # 0-944383-42-4 (hardcover)
ISBN # 0-944383-41-6 (softcover)
Library of Congress Card # 97-71316

———————

ACKNOWLEDGEMENTS

The editor relied upon the writings of Wallace E. Clayton (publisher of the national edition of *The Tombstone Epitaph* newspaper) and the research collections he assembled for much of the information about John Clum included in the introduction and epilogue to this book. The works of Pat M. Ryan were consulted often. Ben T. Traywick (Tombstone's City Historian) was very helpful, as was Edwin R. Sweeney (Cochise's biographer), Tombstone researcher and John Ringo biographer Steve Gatto, and Lynn R. Bailey of Westernlore Press.

CONTENTS

Editor's Introduction 1

Part I: John Clum's Autobiography, 1877-1887

1. Newspapers and Stage Robbers 13

2. The Trek to Tombstone 23

3. Geronimo Breaks Loose 48

4. The Earp-Clanton Battle.................................... 54

5. Adieu to the Earps 68

6. Booms and Depressions 78

Editor's Epilogue 87

Part II: John Clum and the Apaches

7. The Capture of Geronimo................................ 101

8. Apaches as Thespians..................................... 135

Notes and Citations... 157

Sources and References...................................... 164

Index.. 180

MAPS

Arizona settlements circa 1878 12

Tombstone and vicinity circa 1880 24

Downtown Tombstone circa 1881-1882................ 55

*John Clum and Apache leaders Diablo (left) and Eskiminzin.
Photo taken about 1875. John P. Clum Collection, Special
Collections Department, University of Arizona Library.*

EDITOR'S INTRODUCTION

Arizona has a rich history filled with notable events, but two sagas stand out above the others: the Apache wars and the Tombstone silver boom. As a young man John Clum (1851-1932) was importantly involved in both. He was the Indian agent at the San Carlos Apache Reservation from 1874 to 1877 and came to know many Apache leaders well—Eskiminzin was his friend and Geronimo his implacable foe. Clum lived at Tombstone on and off from 1880 to 1886. He was the town's mayor during the turbulent year of 1881 and founder of the *Tombstone Epitaph* newspaper. In Tombstone he became a friend and supporter of lawmen Wyatt and Virgil Earp and an enemy of rustler Ike Clanton.

A few months before his death in Los Angeles at the age of eighty, John Clum began writing an autobiography. He did not complete the project, but he had finished telling the story of his Arizona adventures before a sudden heart attack ended his life. Woodworth Clum (1878-1946), John Clum's only son, found the manuscript on his father's desk. There were twenty-two chapters. The first fourteen covered the period up through 1877 when Clum resigned as Indian agent. Woodworth decided to prepare this portion of the autobiography for publication. However, he went far beyond editing the manuscript. He reworked the early chapters, added bits and pieces of later ones, and thus constructed a *biography* of his father told in the third-person. His book, titled *Apache Agent: The Story of John P. Clum*, was published in 1936. In a preface to the work Woodworth told readers how he altered his father's account: "These [*his father's writings*] I have amplified from the stories he loved to tell; from the tales of other pioneers." The biography concentrates on the Apache wars and only touches on Clum's later experiences. In fact, the first one hundred pages of *Apache Agent* are devoted to a discussion of Apache troubles that took place before Clum's arrival in the Southwest.

The present whereabouts of the first fourteen chapters of John Clum's autobiography is not known. Luckily, the subsequent chapters of the manuscript have survived and now are in the Special Collections Department of the University of Arizona Library. Marjorie Clum Parker (Woodworth Clum's daughter) donated her grandfather's papers to the library in 1955. The portion of the autobiography in which John Clum tells of his life in Arizona after leaving his post at the San Carlos Reservation is published here for the first time. Although he was in his eighty-first year when he composed these reminiscences, his spirit was as youthful and enthusiastic as when he first arrived in the Southwest at the age of twenty.

John Clum's Early Life

John Philip Clum was born September 1, 1851, at his parents' farm near Claverack, New York. As were many folk who lived in the beautiful Hudson River Valley, the Clums were of Dutch stock. William H. and Elizabeth Van Deusen Clum raised a large brood of children, six boys and three girls. They weren't wealthy, but they managed to send John to the nearby Hudson River Institute, a military academy and prep school. After graduation John, in deference to his parents' wishes, enrolled in the divinity program at Rutgers College in New Brunswick, New Jersey. At that time Rutgers was affiliated with the Dutch Reformed Church (the school has since been secularized). In the fall of 1870 Clum, a sturdily-built, five-foot-nine athlete, played for Rutgers against a team from Princeton in a curious new game called "football." This was the second time men from the two schools had squared off in a football contest. There were twenty-five players on each side, the rules were vague, and it was difficult to determine who won. But the rugged football player was not immune to illness. Toward the end of his freshman year at Rutgers a serious rheumatic condition flared up that forced Clum to abandon his athletic pursuits. Fortunately, a summer of rest at home restored his vigor.

As the fall of 1871 approached, John Clum made a decision that would change his life dramatically. He had no burning desire to resume his divinity studies and become a parson, and money for college tuition was scarce. Farming did not appeal to him. Then an intriguing opportunity arose. Clum learned that the U.S. Army Signal Service (now known as the Signal Corps) had been assigned the task of establishing fifty weather stations throughout the states and territories and was recruiting men to staff them. Here was a chance to leave the tame Hudson River Valley and, hopefully, head West, where opportunities seemed unlimited. On September 14, 1871, Clum joined the Signal Service. After six weeks of training at Fort Whipple (later renamed Fort Myer) in Virginia, Clum was given the title of "Observer Sergeant" and sent to New Mexico as a weatherman.

John Clum was stationed in the old city of Santa Fe, and there

John Clum as a Rutgers College freshman. John P. Clum Collection, Special Collections Department, University of Arizona Library.

he faithfully tended to his thermometer, rain gauge, and barometer. He sent his readings to Washington by telegraph. But even at this early date young John had more than one iron in the fire. He organized a private school and in his spare time taught the children of the town's elite. Tuition was three dollars per month per pupil, and when the student body grew to seventy-five he had to hire an assistant. New Mexico governor Marsh Giddings took a liking to John and on one occasion asked him to stay in the Palace of the Governors while he was on an extended trip to the States. Of course Clum was only a "house-sitter," but while occupying Giddings' suite his friends cheerfully addressed him as "Governor."

While in Santa Fe Clum joined the Presbyterian Church—there were no Dutch Reformed congregations in the Southwest. Clum was sincere but not unpleasantly pious in his religious beliefs, and he even developed a few minor "vices." Marjorie Parker recalled that in later years her grandfather enjoyed his evening cocktails and, in true newspaper reporter fashion, smoked Lucky Strike cigarettes.

As Clum's tour of duty with the Signal Service was nearing an end, another position was opening up. The Office of Indian

Affairs (now known as the Bureau of Indian Affairs) needed an agent to supervise the San Carlos Apache Reservation in Arizona. The reserve had been established on the middle reach of the Gila River in 1872, but up to this time the management of San Carlos had been haphazard and ineffectual. Finding the right man to take charge of the remote reservation occupied by the feared Apaches was not easy.

In large part Clum's appointment to the San Carlos post was made possible by President Ulysses S. Grant's "Indian peace policy" then in effect. The policy was based upon recommendations made to Grant by a group of Quakers who had embarked on a crusade to solve the "Indian problem" and end the bloodshed that was a daily occurrence on the Western frontier. The major thrusts of the plan were: 1. Settle the nomadic tribes on reservations and teach them how to be self-sufficient farmers. 2. Introduce the Indians to Christianity and thus elevate them spiritually and cleanse them of their barbaric habits. 3. As Indian-White hostilities subside (and they will when the Indians become Christianized farmers), reduce the role of the military on the Western reservations. The president and his advisors hoped that eventually the Office of Indian Affairs, a bureau within the Department of the Interior, eventually could take full responsibility for the native tribes and the lands set aside for them. Civilian agents would implement the Indian Bureau's policies on the reservations, and Christian religious organizations would be enlisted to assist the Bureau in locating men with high moral standards for these assignments. In response to the president's plan, a number of church groups became involved in recruiting Indian agents.

As chance would have it, the Dutch Reformed Church was the denomination responsible for finding a man to serve at San Carlos. Church officials contacted Rutgers College to see if a student or recent graduate might be interested in the job. Some of Clum's old classmates mentioned that Clum, the former divinity student, was already out West and would be an ideal candidate for Apache agent. The Indian Bureau, at the suggestion of the churchmen, contacted Clum, and in February 1874 he accepted their offer. He was only twenty-two years old. After a few months of instruction in Washington, Clum headed for the Apache country, arriving at San Carlos in August 1874. The Apaches gave their new agent the name "Nantan-betunnykahyeh" or "Boss-with-the-high-forehead." Clum was becoming bald, a condition unknown among young Apache men, and, to the Indians, Clum's shiny pate was his most distinctive feature.

"Good" Apaches, "Bad" Apaches, and Jealous Generals

The ambitious young Indian agent took the policy of demilitarizing reservations seriously. Upon assuming his post at San Carlos, Clum set about learning the Apaches' ways and needs and did not ask the military authorities for protection or advice. Nothing short of a state of war existed between the Apaches and White settlers and soldiers, but Clum was undaunted. He soon demanded that the army withdraw from the immediate vicinity of the reservation and leave the Apaches totally in his hands. His request was granted in October 1875. To keep peace among the various Apache groups and to apprehend wrongdoers, Clum established a native police force. The only non-Apache in the outfit was its leader, Clay Beauford (the real name of this remarkable former soldier and Medal of Honor winner was Welford Bridwell). His Apache policemen proved to be capable and loyal. Native judges, appointed by Clum, determined the guilt of individuals charged with crimes and, if guilty, specified their punishments. Clum hired another ex-soldier, Martin A. Sweeney, as his administrative assistant. Sweeney was efficient, got on well with the Apaches, and kept things running smoothly when Clum was away. In the spring of 1875 John Clum brought an older brother, George A. Clum (1849-1935), to the reservation and he taught school there for a term. (George Clum taught school at Florence for two years. Then in 1878 he moved to Tucson, where he studied law and worked as a clerk in the court system. He was part owner of the *Arizona Citizen* newspaper in Tucson from 1884 to 1890. Later he moved to Mesilla, New Mexico.) Clum set about training his charges to be farmers. He placed the Apaches in encampments along the streams and showed them how to put the fertile bottom land to cultivation. The farms were productive and corn harvests were impressive. But Clum outlawed the production of *tiswin*, a homemade corn beer. His policemen arrested thirsty residents who defied the ban. Clum's regimen included other restrictions: no Apache could leave the reservation without special permission; men had to present themselves to be counted daily and women and children were counted each Saturday; only policemen could possess firearms, etc. Clum was proud of his system, which he considered to be "self-rule" for the Apaches. Even so, the Indian police and judges were allowed only to enforce the rules—they had no say in making them.

Naturally, the military men did not appreciate the brash kid who thought he knew more than they did about dealing with the Apaches. Clum was constantly at odds with Brigadier General George Crook and even more so with Brevet Major General August Kautz, who replaced Crook as commander of the Department of Arizona in the spring of 1875. Military officers don't like to yield their authority to young civilian upstarts under any circumstances, but Crook and Kautz were especially incensed by the constant stream of tactless letters Clum sent to them, to Washington officials, and to the press.

Much to the amazement and irritation of the military, Clum was quite successful in maintaining an orderly, functional reservation. He truly liked and respected "good" Apaches, those who were peaceful and amenable to his rules and regimentation. The "bad" Apaches, the free spirits who longed for the old nomadic life and the raiding that was an integral part of it, were another matter. Clum regarded these restless renegades as criminals who should be jailed or hung. To Clum, the military always seemed insensitive and impatient with the good Apaches and too lenient with the bad ones. And the "baddest" of the bad ones was Geronimo.

John Clum became the focal point of the Indian Bureau's new policy of concentrating the various Apache groups at a single location. Because of the "wonder boy's" success in maintaining order by using native police and because there was good farmland and ample water at the site, Washington officials decided San Carlos was the best place for a megareservation. Clum agreed. One by one, Apache bands from remote sections of Arizona and southwestern New Mexico were brought to San Carlos and placed under his watchful eye. During Clum's first year as Apache agent the number of people under his authority increased from about 800 to more than 4,000. In the end this policy proved to be a mistake. Apaches from distant locales detested living in a strange place with strange neighbors. The people we call Apaches were not a unified nation with a single leadership structure, but were a collection of autonomous groups loosely linked by language and other cultural traits. Some of the bands had long histories of mutual antagonism, and old disputes surfaced when they found themselves living close together.

In the spring of 1876 violence broke out on the Chiricahua Apache Reservation in southeastern Arizona, the home of two of the three Chiricahua bands in existence at that time. Although only a few warriors were involved, Washington authorities

John Clum and Apaches. Photo taken about 1875. John P. Clum Collection, Special Collections Department, University of Arizona Library.

promptly abolished the reservation and ordered Clum to bring the Chiricahuas to San Carlos. He and a team of fifty-four San Carlos police rounded up some three hundred members of the "Central Chiricahua" band led by Cochise's son Taza (Cochise had died in 1874). But the "Southern Chiricahuas" gave Clum's policemen the slip. Led by Juh, Geronimo, and Nolgee, they crossed the border and vanished into the Sierra Madre. The Chiricahua Apaches were especially unsuited to life at San Carlos, which was outside their traditional territory. To these non-agricultural people used to subsisting on wild plants and animals and plunder taken from their neighbors, the place was nothing more than a prison. Again and again during the next decade they would flee the reservation and go on the warpath.

In July 1876 John Clum took time out from his hectic responsibilities and returned to the East to visit family and consult with his superiors. But he had other fish to fry as well. With him were twenty-two Apaches—sixteen men, four women, and two boys—and Clum planned to make a few dollars putting on a "Wild Indian Show." The production made its debut at the Olympic Theatre in St. Louis. But the exhibition of Apache lifeways and warfare techniques did not go over as well as Clum had hoped. Only a few weeks had elapsed since the Sioux massacred General George Custer's command in Montana, and the nation was still in mourning. As a result, few people were inclined to pay money to hobnob with "wild" Indians, no matter how exciting their presentation might be. Clum's first show business experiment was a monetary bust. However, he did demonstrate to Indian Affairs officials that Apaches were people, not demons. Unfortunately, the trip was marred by the death of Taza. He succumbed to pneumonia while the group was in Washington and was buried in the Congressional Cemetery there.

Clum and his companions visited the Centennial Exposition at Philadelphia, then he and the Apaches headed for home. The train took them to El Moro, Colorado, where wagons and teamsters from San Carlos were waiting. Clum, confident that the party could travel the rest of the way on their own, left the group and backtracked to Delaware, Ohio. (Delaware is a few miles north of Columbus.) There, on November 8, 1876, he married Mary Dennison Ware. Exactly how the two became acquainted is uncertain. They courted by letter. Mary was a member of a well-to-do and politically influential family. Her uncle, William H. Dennison, had served a term as governor of Ohio and was postmaster general during the Lincoln administration. Mary lost her father, Thomas D. Ware, when she was very young and her uncle became her guardian. Clum's connection to the Dennisons gave him an inside track to Postal Service jobs, and he would take advantage of this in the future. After a short honeymoon in San Francisco, Clum and his bride made their way to San Carlos. By all accounts Mary, whose nickname was "Mollie," was a vivacious, outgoing young woman.

Despite being recruited by church officials, many Indian agents of the period were men whose only interest was lining their own pockets. By contrast Clum was honest, dedicated, and possessed boundless energy. He defended peaceful Apaches against injustices and spent long days in the saddle in pursuit of

Mary Ware, soon to become Mary Clum. John P. Clum Collection, Special Collections Department, University of Arizona Library.

troublemakers. One of his most celebrated achievements occurred in April 1877 when he, Clay Beauford, and about one hundred Apache policemen arrested Geronimo near the Ojo Caliente (Warm Springs) Reservation in New Mexico. The Chiricahua warlord and a number of his followers were taken into custody without a shot being fired. The only resistance was offered by an enraged Apache woman who charged forward and, with a defiant war cry, leaped on Beauford and tried to take away his rifle. But everyone kept calm, the woman was restrained, and Geronimo was placed in irons and taken to San Carlos. Victorio and his "Eastern Chiricahua" band were brought from Ojo Caliente to San Carlos at the same time. The Ojo Caliente Reservation was then decommissioned and the land returned to the public domain.

Clum believed Geronimo was a robber and murderer and wanted him tried as a criminal. But despite his reputation, there was little evidence that would hold up in court linking Geronimo directly to specific crimes. Nonetheless, the Apache leader was still shackled when Clum, disillusioned and tired of feuding with the military, resigned as agent for San Carlos in July 1877.

Many writers have attempted to assess Clum's performance as Apache agent. Most give him high marks, but others point out that the cocky young man didn't understand the Apaches as well as he thought he did, and therefore his programs, which seemed to work at first, ultimately failed. There is some truth in this criticism, but, in reality, his job was an impossible one. Nomadic Apaches and White settlers were incompatible. No one was savvy enough to devise a plan that would accommodate both groups and allow both cultures to flourish side-by-side. As a result, the reservation system did not bring peace, and Apache-White relations continued to be sorted out on the battlefield. But compared to other Indian agents of the time, Clum was one of the most able men to work for the Office of Indian Affairs.

The next phase of John Clum's life is described in the following chapters in his own words. Still very young (twenty-five years old), he found himself without employment and with a wife to support. But he had no lack of self-confidence. Upon relinquishing his job with the Indian Bureau, Clum left San Carlos and moved to Tucson, and there is where his story begins . . . .

PART I

John Clum's Autobiography, 1877-1887

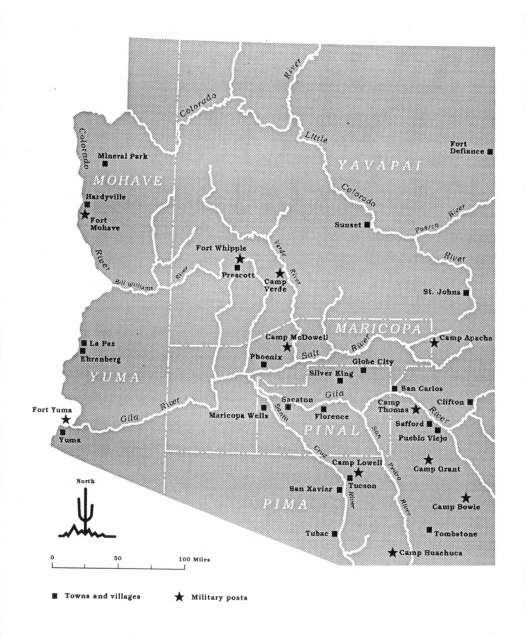

Arizona settlements circa 1878. Map drawn by Sid Alwin.

1

NEWSPAPERS AND STAGE ROBBERS

Tucson in 1877 . . . midsummer . . . a wife . . . and no job. During spare time at the [*San Carlos Apache*] agency I had read law, so why not become a lawyer? I shopped around amongst my lawyer friends, looking for an opening where I could complete my studies and acquire some practical experience. Before I got located, Judge H. B. Summers of Florence, Arizona, offered me a partnership with him. He was an outstanding member of the Arizona bar and helped me greatly in my efforts to become a lawyer. I was admitted to practice on November 16th, less than five months after resigning as Indian agent.

Florence was a small frontier town [*about seventy miles north of Tucson*], and the law business was not consuming all of my time. [*Florence, the Pinal County seat, was home to about eight hundred people.*] My life with the Apaches had been full of action and thrills. Sitting in an office and looking out the window at the desert sagebrush while waiting for a client were not sufficiently exciting. So I promoted a newspaper. Florence had no newspaper and I thought it needed one. Four or five business men of Florence liked the idea. We made an oral agreement of partnership and purchased the "Arizona Citizen" then being published at Tucson. [*Clum bought the paper from Rollin C. Brown and John Wasson.[1] After the sale Brown moved to Florence and worked for Clum as a printer.[2]*]

We removed the plant and equipment to Florence. I had begun the construction of a residence at the north end of the village, and it was approaching completion when the "Citizen" plant arrived from Tucson. Inasmuch as no other suitable building was available, I transformed my contemplated residence into a printing office and the "Arizona Citizen" was duly established in that building. For reasons which I do not now definitely recall, the oral agreement with my partners in the newspaper enterprise soon developed into a disagreement and I found myself sole proprietor of a weekly newspaper. In order to protect my investment, it became necessary for me to suspend the study and practice of law and devote my entire energies to the job of publishing the first newspaper in Pinal County. [*The first issue of the Florence* Citizen *appeared November 9, 1877.[3]*]

The Arizona Citizen *office in Tucson circa 1890. John Clum bought the paper in 1877 and sold it in 1880. In 1884 his brother George Clum became part owner of the* Citizen. *Arizona Historical Society, Tucson, #2867.*

◇ ◇ ◇ ◇ ◇

In July 1878 I was returning from a business trip to Tucson via the stage, a small two-seated affair drawn by two horses. A veterinary surgeon from Fort Lowell [*located about seven miles east of Tucson*] occupied the rear seat with me, while a Chinaman was perched on the box with the driver. My traveling costume of that period included a Colt's 45 and a belt of cartridges. The veterinary was equipped with two six-shooters. The driver also had a six-gun. We left Tucson shortly after noon, and as it was pretty warm I threw my coat and vest on the front seat, unbuckled my belt, and placed it, with the six-shooter, on the floor of the coach. The veterinary merely loosened his belt. There had not been a stage robbery on this route for about seven years, consequently we had no thought of trouble.

Eighteen miles northwest of Tucson, at Point of Rocks, we were moving slowly through heavy sand. Abruptly the coach stopped and there appeared at the left door a stalwart form wearing a broad hat, a coat turned wrong side out, and a bandanna handkerchief drawn across the lower part of his face. This picturesque costume gave the stranger a decidedly comical appearance, but I soon discovered that he meant business. He held at his shoulder a Sharps [*Spencer*] carbine capable of discharging seven fifty-caliber bullets in rapid succession. The thumb of his right hand had already drawn back the hammer of the carbine, and the index finger was toying with the trigger. His left hand supported the barrel of the rifle, and the fingers of that hand grasped the cylinder of a Colt's 45, thus holding the barrel of that six-gun parallel with the barrel of the carbine. Both of those barrels were directed at my midsection. And he had an additional six-shooter in its scabbard at his hip.

He commanded us to "Stick 'em up!" My six-shooter on the floor of the coach might as well have been in Tucson or Timbuctoo, so far as its immediate use as a weapon of defense was concerned. Realizing that we were in the midst of a genuine stage robbery, my first thought was for the safety of my new watch and chain. Instead of complying with his command to "stick 'em up," I dropped my right hand on the watch chain and drew it further out of the robber's vision. This annoyed him exceedingly and he exclaimed, "Don't fold your hands. Hold 'em up or I'll kill you deader'n hell!" Certain nervous movements of his thumb and finger about the hammer and trigger of the carbine convinced me that the highwayman was either excited or in earnest, and that in either case my life might be in jeopardy. Therefore, I gave the watch chain another yank to the right and then promptly "stuck 'em up." In the meantime, the veterinary waved both hands out of the stage door.

In order that we might clearly understand his viewpoint, the robber said, "If you want to fight, begin shooting. You may get me, but I'll get some of you first, and I'd just as soon die as not." This statement was absolutely sincere, as we learned later. At the robber's command, the driver threw out the mail and express. The Chinaman disgorged a few dollars. Then the robber advised me to pass over my valuables. I had only three Mexican dollars in my pants—what little real money I had was in my coat and vest. I reached for two dollars in my right-hand pocket, at the same time maneuvering the watch chain still further out of his vision. When I threw out the two dollars, the robber registered intense indignation, so I dug into the left pocket for the third dollar, whereupon he insisted I had my wealth concealed in a money belt. He was not satisfied until I demonstrated to him that I was not wearing such a belt. However, this demonstration was made on the left side, opposite the watch pocket. As the watch was not demanded, I decided not to present it. The robber was most disagreeable and indicated his inclination to kill me on general principles. Then he turned his attention to the veterinary and compelled him to contribute some $30.

After my return to Florence, my friends got quite a kick out of facetious inquiries regarding the stage robbery. Among these was John Miller, justice of the peace, formerly a deputy sheriff with an enviable record. When I met Miller, a conversation something like this followed:

"Hello, Clum. I hear you've been to Tucson."

"Yeah."

"What's the news?"

"Nothing particular."

"Any excitement on the trip home?"

"Nothing particular."

"Oh well, Clum, you're all right when you have a bunch of ragged Indians to deal with, but I notice a lone stage robber makes you throw up your hands."

"I guess you're right, Miller," I replied. "It looked that way to me."

The next week Miller went to Tucson and collected $300, which he had about his person when he took passage on the stage-coach for Florence. Miller rode on the box with the driver. Arriving at Point-of-Rocks, Miller asked, "Where did that robbery occur last week?" "Just a little ahead," the driver replied. "Right there. See that bush . . . why, there he is again!" "Yes, here I am again. Throw up your hands!" was the bandit's greeting, and he proceeded to collect from Miller the three hundred dollars Miller had collected in Tucson. Naturally, that made Miller pretty sore. The next evening I strolled into his office:

"Hello, Miller," I said. "I hear you've been to Tucson."

"Yeah."

"What's the news?"

"Nothing particular."

"Anything exciting on the trip home?"

"Nothing particular."

"Oh well, Miller, you are all right as a cop in town with your gang around you when a lonesome guy drops in for a little celebration, but I notice one lone stage robber makes you throw up your hands."

Miller frowned and murmured something about my going to hell or someplace. For a long time thereafter, a familiar greeting among friends in Florence was, "Here I am again. Throw up your hands." The robber later was identified as William "Billy" Brazelton who had pulled off several stage robberies in southern Arizona. He was killed by a sheriff's posse a few days later [*on August 19, 1878[4]*].

The stage robber William Brazelton in death. He is holding a Remington rolling block carbine. Photo taken in Tucson by Henry Buehman. Arizona Historical Society, Tucson, #78140.

◇ ◇ ◇ ◇ ◇

For a novice editor and proprietor of a newspaper, I succeeded fairly well but soon realized that Florence was not a particularly profitable location. So I removed to Tucson and during the autumn [*September*] of 1878 resumed the publication of the weekly "Citizen" at the place of its birth. [*The* Arizona Citizen *was founded at Tucson in 1870 by John Wasson and Richard C. McCormick.5*] The Southern Pacific Railroad recently had entered Arizona at Yuma and construction of tracks was being rapidly pushed toward Tucson. Although Tucson was still an isolated frontier community with a population of about 5,000 composed largely of Mexicans, the approach of the railroad gave promise of substantial progress in the near future. I determined that my newspaper should anticipate this promised development, and, accordingly, in February 1879 I established the "Daily Arizona Citizen" at Tucson, the first daily newspaper published in Arizona.

[*The Southern Pacific tracks reached Tucson from the west in the spring of 1880 and were completed across Arizona later that year. By March 1881 passengers and freight were being transported over the nation's second transcontinental rail system.6*

Clum's Citizen *was the first Arizona newspaper to successfully publish as a daily. The* Arizona Star *(Tucson) tried daily publication in March 1877 (as the* Daily Bulletin*) and again in January 1879, but on both occasions soon reverted to a weekly format. The* Star *became a full-fledged daily in June 1879.7*]

Tucson was still an adobe town with not more than a dozen two-story structures—nearly all buildings were one story with flat, mud roofs. The first shingle roof on any private residence in Tucson was the one I had put on the home I built for my little family, which, by the way, now included a baby boy.

[*Woodworth Clum was born on October 20, 1878. The Clum's first child, a boy, died in infancy. In the summer of 1879 Mary Clum took Woodworth back to Ohio to show him off to relatives. Several letters she wrote to her husband during her lengthy visit survive. In them she indicated that she preferred Ohio, with its green trees, flowers, social life, and comforts, to Arizona. But Mary emphasized that her fondest desire was to live with John, wherever he might be. In a letter dated June 18, 1879, she wrote: "I think of our life at San Carlos and it is like a dream. It sends a*

Mary and John Clum. John P. Clum Collection, Special Collections Department, University of Arizona Library.

shudder through me to think of the horrible Indians and the lonely place. Yet I was contented."[8]]

Tucson was treeless and verdureless; there was no water for irrigation purposes within the city limits. All water for domestic purposes was brought in daily in carts [*from nearby springs*], and each family was supplied by the bucketful. There were several Chinese laundries in town, but the greater portion of the laundry was done by Mexican women who took the clothes down to the Santa Cruz River where there was ample water for cleansing purposes.

Alex Levin maintained a brewery and amusement park where, among other things, he provided a dancing floor and Mexican orchestra. Here the American element of the city assembled in considerable numbers during those delightful summer nights. Dances were mostly old-fashioned quadrilles but provided entertainment quite as thrilling and healthful as the dances of today.

During 1879 the Globe mining district was developing into a region of importance with a rapidly growing population. The citizens of Tucson felt they were entitled to their share of the trade with that community, but there was no highway between Tucson and Globe [*located about one hundred miles to the north*]. It was determined that a road must be constructed, and W. [*Wheeler*] W. Williams, Mariano Samaniego, and I were appointed road commissioners charged with the construction of a road from Tucson to the site of old Camp Grant on the lower Rio San Pedro and thence down the San Pedro valley to the Gila. This part of the new highway offered few obstacles, but the section through the mountains, from the Gila to Globe, interposed many difficulties. But the task was accomplished and the road was in condition for acceptance by the middle of December 1879. We built a road, but, I fear, compared with modern standards it should have been labeled "Dangerous but Passable." This was the first highway constructed by civilians in Arizona.

Tucson, owing to its remote location and lack of proper transportation, had depended upon local talent for its entertainment. In November 1879 we brought in a professional opera troupe which presented the comic opera [*"H.M.S."*] "Pinafore." The initial performance was a red-letter night in the social development of Tucson.

As an official of the Presbyterian Church at Tucson, I took an active part in the erection of the first Protestant church built in southern Arizona—probably the first in Arizona. [*Construction began on the adobe church in June 1878, and it was completed the next year.*[9]]

Looking north on Tucson's Meyer Street in the spring of 1880. The first Protestant church (Presbyterian) built in Arizona can be seen in the background at the left. Carleton Watkins photo, Arizona Historical Society, Tucson, #14843.

On January 29, 1880, I participated in the first, last, and only sleigh ride ever witnessed in Tucson. Snow began falling about 6 p.m. the previous evening and continued until about noon that day, during which time eight inches had fallen. [*An 8" snowfall in the desert city of Tucson is a very rare event.*] Two carpenters speedily transformed some 2 X 4 scantlings into a set of "runners." A de-wheeled farm wagon was attached and our sleigh was in readiness. A prancing four-in-hand team from Bob Leatherwood's corral, bells jingling, completed the outfit. The story had been noised about town and a goodly throng assembled. With two other young men and our three best girls we climbed into the contrivance and were off amid the cheers—and jeers—of the multitude. Unfortunately, we had been compelled to devote precious hours to preparations, and the Arizona sun was breaking through the clouds. After a trek through the city streets, we drove out on the stage road toward Picacho. Soon the normal Tucson temperature transformed the snow into slush. We turned about, set our gear in low, and slid back home in the mud. Nevertheless, we developed a novel idea, entertained the public, established a record that still stands, provided human interest news items for the "Citizen," and had lots of real fun.

2

THE TREK TO TOMBSTONE

A new shibboleth [*catchword*] intrigued the Southwest during the winter of 1879-80. Ed Schieffelin had discovered TOMBSTONE. Over desert mountains, through desert valleys, a nondescript horde followed the trails to this newest Mecca of the hopeful. It must have been a prospector, with his burro and his gold pan, his bacon and his flour, that the poet had in mind when he said, "Hope springs eternal." Ed Schieffelin was such a prospector. For years he had searched the hills of Arizona in vain. In July '77 he was down at Camp Huachuca, broke but hopeful. One afternoon he packed his burro and hiked out over the hills. Two months later, Al Sieber, army scout, met Ed on the trail near the San Pedro River. [*The following conversation is folklore.*]

"How's things, Al?"

"So so, Ed. Found your mine yet?"

"Naw," drawled Ed, "but I just found a pretty good looking stone up thar on that hillside."

"If you don't quit wandering around these mountains," replied Al, "the Apaches'll git you and all you'll find will be your tombstone."

"Mebbe," said Ed.

"So long," said Al, and he resumed the trail to Tucson. Ed went back to the hillside and discovered a ledge of pure silver. When he filed his claim and named his mine, he remembered what Al Sieber had said and called it "Tombstone." News of the discovery flashed all over the western country. Miners, gamblers, merchants, outlaws, women (both of the wild and domestic varieties), all headed for Tombstone. A city grew over night.

Business in Tucson began to lag, so in December '79 I rode over to Tombstone and sized it up carefully. Business was booming; the future seemed alluring. Returning to Tucson, I sold the "Citizen" to R. C. Brown on February 2, 1880, and moved, bag and baggage, to this promising new El Dorado. Also, I had made arrangements to have a small newspaper press, some type, and all the other necessary newspaper equipment sent by wagon freight. Pending its arrival, I had nothing in particular to do except

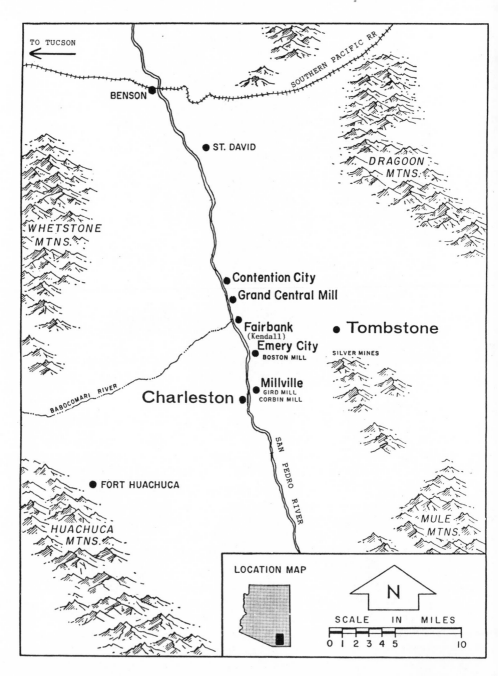

*Tombstone and vicinity circa 1880. Adapted from a map drawn by
Don Bufkin.*

Ed Schieffelin, discoverer of the Tombstone mines. The prospector is shown with a fine Sharps rifle. C. S. Fly photo, Arizona Historical Society, Tucson, #26483.

select a name for my new publication. [*Rollin C. Brown became a part owner of the* Citizen *shortly before he bought Clum out entirely. In an unpublished memoir Brown noted: "I used to get out of patience with Clum. He was brainy enough but . . . neglected things."*]

During the past 50 years many stories have been published attributing the suggestion of the name "The Epitaph" to various persons active in the life of early Tombstone. I'm sorry, very sorry, to spoil these legends, but the simple truth is that I figured it out all by myself. Certainly it was no flash of genius, as some folks seem to think. From time immemorial the written epitaph and the monumental tombstone have been in intimate mental as well as physical contact. The thought that a newspaper to be published in the "City of Tombstone" should be called "The Epitaph" would occur spontaneously in the mind of anyone possessing either a moderate sense of humor or an appreciation of the eternal fitness of things.

The business public of Tombstone was deeply interested in the establishment of a new paper, but popular approval of the proposed name was by no means unanimous. My critics included personal friends whose objections and misgivings were sincere and could not be overruled in an arbitrary or flippant manner. "The Tombstone Epitaph," they quoted. Could the paper prosper or even survive having such a handicap in its name? Was it a proper title under which to proclaim this vast mineral district to the world? What would be the psychological effect of sending a local paper with such a name to friends in the states? Would the press of the country commend or ridicule "The Tombstone Epitaph?" One day in Tucson I met my good friend John Wasson, surveyor general of Arizona and former editor and proprietor of the "Arizona Citizen." He was my senior by forty years. "Clum," he said, "I understand you have practically decided to name your new paper 'The Tombstone Epitaph.'" I cheerfully confirmed his worst fears. "Don't do it," he pleaded. "That name will kill the paper within six months. I think Tombstone offers a most promising field for a good paper. I want you to succeed. Take my advice and don't name your paper 'The Epitaph.'"

In discussing the subject with the dissenters I always evinced an optimistic mood, which, indeed, was genuine. A pet argument was my belief that the name would yield to the paper, and to Tombstone, a million dollars worth of free advertizing within six months. Every paragrapher and wit in the country would lie awake at night creating more or less smart quips relative to the new journal which had made its appearance in the midst of the wide open spaces of the great Southwest. Furthermore, the mining district had prospered under the name of "Tombstone," and by the same token the paper would prosper under the unique title of "The Epitaph." The first issue was published May 1, 1880. Throughout more than a half-century, "The Tombstone Epitaph" has carried on its name with varying degrees of literary and financial success, while its title has spread its fame to the far-flung corners of the civilized world. It still survives.

Our temporary canvas home was erected on the rear of a lot,

but very soon the stout adobe walls of a two-story building began to arise on the front of the lot. Within a few weeks all equipment and printing material were transferred from the humble canvas birthplace to the more substantial and commodious quarters in the new building, which is still standing.

A group of musicians pose in Fremont Street. The Epitaph *office is behind them—in the two-story building to the right of the assay office. Photo taken about 1885. Arizona Historical Society, Tucson, #79293.*

[*Although Clum did not mention him, he had a partner, Thomas R. Sorin, who helped found the* Epitaph. *Clum did most of the writing and editing, and Sorin took care of the printing chores. A third partner, Charles D. Reppy, joined Clum and Sorin in October 1880. Sorin sold out to Clum and left the* Epitaph *in April 1881.[1]*

The Tombstone Epitaph, *a periodical too tough to die, survived as a weekly when Clum wrote his memoir, and it is with us today. At present the paper is published in two formats. A monthly "national edition" features articles of historical interest and has subscribers throughout the world. A biweekly "local edition," produced as a class project by the students of the University of Arizona Department of Journalism, keeps Tombstone residents abreast of current happenings about town. This edition is not published during the summer months.*

COL. JOHN P. CLUM.

MAJ. THOMAS SORIN.

CAPT. CHARLES D. REPPY.

The "officers" of the Epitaph. Arizona Quarterly Illustrated,
January 1881.

Tombstone's first newspaper was the Weekly Nugget *founded by Artemus E. Fay. The inaugural issue of the* Nugget *appeared October 2, 1879. The paper became the* Tombstone Daily Nugget *in the fall of 1880.[2] The* Nugget *was Democratic in political orientation, Clum's paper Republican. Unlike the* Epitaph, *the* Nugget *was short lived—the newspaper went out of business after its print shop was destroyed by fire on May 25, 1882.*]

Richard (Dick) Gird was the first postmaster at Tombstone. [*Gird was appointed postmaster on December 2, 1878.[3]*] He was also Ed [*and Albert*] Schieffelin's partner and owned valuable interests in a mine located by Ed in 1878. In the spring of 1880 Gird disposed of his mining interests in Tombstone for a half million dollars and decided to resign as postmaster and locate in southern California. But a successor was necessary before he could quit his post office job. I was selected as the victim and in July succeeded Dick as postmaster at Tombstone.

[*According to U.S. Postal Service records Gird resigned as postmaster in early May 1880, and George Perine served for about a month before Clum was appointed postmaster on June 4 (Clum took charge of the post office on July 1).[4] However, Gird did not leave the area at that time. His partners, Ed and Al Schieffelin, sold their mining interests in the spring of 1880 (reportedly for $600,000, a huge fortune in those days), but Gird retained his Tombstone properties until the spring of 1881. He then sold out for about the same sum his partners had received and left the territory. Gird and the Schieffelins were among the few Tombstone pioneers wise enough to cash in and get out while the getting was good.[5]*]

The rush was on. I removed and refitted the post office three times within a year in an endeavor to keep pace with the rapid growth of the community. Tombstone was now the largest city in Arizona.

[*The oft-repeated statement that at its zenith Tombstone exceeded Tucson in size is in error. The 1880 census reported 2,100 people living in Tombstone and 7,000 in Tucson. A special census taken in Cochise County in 1882, when the silver boom was at its peak, determined that 5,300 people resided in Tombstone. By 1890 Tombstone's population had dwindled to about 1,900. Thus Tucson never lost the distinction of being the largest town in southern Arizona.*]

◇ ◇ ◇ ◇ ◇

Left to right, Richard Gird (1836-1910), Albert Schieffelin (1849-1885), Edward Schieffelin (1847-1897). Arizona Historical Society, Tucson, #22635.

It has come to be legend that we used to kill a man for breakfast every morning in those hectic days in Tombstone. True, the town was tough, but not as tough as that. Of the 15,000 [*5,000*] inhabitants, about 15 were of the two-gun, quick-shootin' variety. The rest of us were perfectly good citizens—lawyers, doctors, mine workers, butchers and bakers and candle-stick makers. And a couple of editors. There is no worldwide news in a church social or an amateur theatrical. The headlines of the world's newspapers, then as now, yearned for a murder story. For this reason, Tombstone has gone down in history with all its bloody episodes generously recorded and its normal life ignored. Well, "The evil that men do lives after them; the good oft is interred with their bones. So let it be with Caesar." And with Tombstone.

Among the newcomers to Tombstone were the Earp brothers, five of them: Virgil, Wyatt, Morgan, Jim, and Warren. Tall, gaunt, intrepid, they caused considerable comment when they first arrived, particularly because of Wyatt's reputation as a peace officer in Dodge City, Kansas. All the cattle rustlers in Kansas, Colorado, New Mexico, and western Texas knew and feared Wyatt Earp. The other brothers knew what six-shooters were used for, too, but Wyatt had the reputation.

[*James, Virgil, and Wyatt Earp arrived in Tombstone with their wives in December 1879.[6] Younger brothers Morgan and Warren Earp came to Arizona some months later. Contrary to Clum's fanciful assertion, Wyatt was not a renowned lawman. He had been employed as an assistant marshal in Dodge City intermittently from 1876 to 1879, but as a city police officer of modest rank he had no opportunity or authority to terrorize rustlers throughout the West.[7] When the Earps showed up in Tombstone only Virgil, a deputy U.S. marshal, was a law enforcement official.[8]*]

Looking west on Tombstone's Allen Street in the spring of 1880. Carleton Watkins photo, Arizona Historical Society, Tucson, #14835.

Another contribution from Dodge City to Tombstone was Doc [*John H.*] Holliday. Doc got his prefix as a dentist. He was born in Georgia, drifted over into Texas, got into trouble in a poker game, and made a getaway to Dodge City. In a Dodge City saloon one day a cattle thief was about to shoot Wyatt in the back, but Doc saw what was going on and killed the cattle thief. Wyatt and Doc Holliday were bosom friends ever afterwards. [*There is no known Dodge City newspaper article or court document corroborating this rustler-shooting story.*]

In fact, most of Tombstone's quick-shootin' population came via Dodge City, including Luke Short, a faro dealer who worked at the Oriental [*an ornate saloon and gambling house run by Milt Joyce and frequented by the Earps and other notables*]. A tough customer from Deadwood, S.D., named [*Charlie*] Storms walked into the Oriental one afternoon, waved a six-shooter under Short's nose, and delivered himself of the opinion that most of those Dodge City reputations were the bunk. Luke pulled his gun and Mr. Storms' funeral was the following day. None questioned Dodge City's reputation after that. [*Luke Short shot Charlie Storms on February 25, 1881.[9] Law enforcement officials deemed the shooting self defense.*]

About this time Johnny Behan drifted into town and announced he had been appointed sheriff for Cochise County, of which Tombstone was now the county seat. Johnny would have been all right back in his native Missouri, but the Tombstone pace was a bit too fast for him. The cattle rustlers and outlaws in Cochise County were too sharp and too quick on the trigger for Johnny. He became too lenient to them and too friendly with them. And he played too much politics. As sheriff, Behan was supposed to stop cattle stealing, stage hold-ups, and similar diversions then prevalent in southeastern Arizona.

[*Clum was staunchly loyal to his old friends. Therefore, his unflattering depiction of John Behan undoubtedly was influenced by the fact that Behan and Clum's hero Wyatt Earp had been rivals and not on good terms. On November 9, 1880, after serving a little more than three months, Wyatt resigned as deputy Pima County sheriff for Tombstone.[10] Pima County Sheriff Charles Shibell appointed John Behan to replace him.[11] On February 1, 1881, the Arizona legislature passed a bill creating Cochise County (with Tombstone as county seat) by splitting off a section of eastern Pima County.[12] It was the governor's duty to appoint the new county's first group of officials, and Wyatt Earp wanted to be sheriff. But Governor John Frémont selected Behan for the*]

John Behan (1845-1912, left) and Wyatt Earp (1848-1929). Wyatt wanted to be Cochise County's first sheriff, but Behan walked off with the prize. Behan was a Democrat. Wyatt's political leanings are less certain (see note 13, page 158). Arizona Historical Society, Tucson, #24740 and #1447.

post. Then Behan reneged on a promise he had made to Wyatt to hire him as his undersheriff or second-in-command. This rankled Earp and helped generate bad blood between the two lawmen.[13]]

The rustler gang had been headed by Old Man [*Newman H.*] Clanton and his three boys, Ike [*Joseph Isaac*], Finn [*Phineas*], and Billy [*William H.*], but the father recently had been killed while on a cattle-stealing expedition into Old Mexico. So the Clanton boys formed an alliance with Tom and Frank McLowery [*McLaury*], who, next to the Clantons, were the leading rustlers in that vicinity. [*In Clum's day most writers spelled Tom and Frank McLaury's last name either "McLowry" or "McLowery." Modern researchers have concluded that "McLaury" is correct.*] The Clanton-McLowery gang, as outlaws, and the Earps, as peace officers, a total of ten men, furnished most of the six-shooter fireworks for which Tombstone became famous. And five of these, the outlaws, were not residents of Tombstone.

[*In August 1881 a large party of Mexicans, probably soldiers, ambushed a group of seven Americans camped in a remote canyon near the point where Arizona, New Mexico, and Sonora converge. Five men, including Old Man Clanton and stage robber*

Jim Crane, were killed, and two men escaped to report the incident. It is assumed that the soldiers attacked the Americans in retribution for crimes they believed Clanton and his companions had committed against Mexican citizens. A few weeks earlier a Mexican pack train had been attacked and several men killed not far from where the Americans were waylaid.[14]

While most authorities agree that the McLaurys and Clantons dealt in cattle of dubious origin from time to time, the extent of their illegal activities is hard to measure. None of them was wanted by the law for rustling, robbery, or some other serious offense at the time of the infamous gunfight in Tombstone. Therefore, they may not have been quite as bad as Clum suggests.]

Harry Schneider, chief engineer at Ed Schieffelin's mine, was walking down Allen Street one morning on his way to work. A gambler known as Johnny-behind-the-deuce bumped into him rather roughly. "Look where you're going," snapped Schneider. Johnny shot from the hip and Schneider fell dead. Instantly the town was in an uproar. Witnesses grabbed Johnny-behind-the-deuce. Within fifteen minutes 500 men had gathered, a rope was obtained, and Johnny was being marched to his own lynching party. Wyatt Earp had been appointed deputy marshal. He heard the hubbub and figured it was his business to prevent the lynching. He arrived just as the rope was being placed around Johnny's neck. Single handed, he cowed the mob and landed Johnny in jail at Tucson.

[Clum's memory let him down in recalling the details of the Johnny-behind-the-deuce saga. An article in the January 17, 1881, issue of the Epitaph *described the incident this way: On January 14, 1881, Johnny-behind-the-deuce shot and killed W. P. Schneider at Charleston, an ore-milling town ten miles west of Tombstone. Schneider was a well-known mining engineer in the employ of Richard Gird (the Schieffelin brothers had sold their Arizona mining properties the previous spring). After the shooting, Johnny was arrested and brought to Tombstone where an angry crowd gathered. The* Epitaph *reported that Ben Sippy (Tombstone's town marshal), Virgil Earp (a deputy U.S. marshal), and Johnny Behan (a deputy Pima County sheriff) kept the mob under control and got the prisoner safely to Tucson, the Pima County seat. Wyatt Earp served as a deputy Pima County sheriff from July to November 1880, but he was no longer a peace officer when Schneider was killed and was not mentioned in the* Epitaph's *story about the event. Johnny-behind-the-deuce escaped from the*

Newman H. "Old Man" Clanton (1816-1881). Was he a vicious outlaw or just a good ol' boy who sometimes had a few "undocumented" cows in his corral? Arizona Historical Society, Tucson, #40882.

Joseph Isaac "Ike" Clanton (1847-1887), arch enemy of the Earps. C. S. Fly photo, Arizona Historical Society, Tucson, #24366.

Tucson jail in April 1881 and was never apprehended.[15]]

◇ ◇ ◇ ◇ ◇

In July 1880 I changed the "Weekly Epitaph" into the "Daily Epitaph." [*Clum continued to publish a weekly edition of the* Epitaph *along with the daily.*] The boom was still on. Feverish development was in progress in every industry within the city and among mines, affording abundant material for our news columns. About the time the "Daily Epitaph" made its appearance, a spirited controversy arose concerning the title of city lots. Title to all lots was claimed by the Townsite Company. A large part of the area of the city was covered by mining locations [*claims*], the owners of which claimed all surface rights for mining purposes. Last, but by no means least, was the individual claimant, the bona fide citizen who claimed title to his lot by right of actual occupancy. The "Epitaph" came out boldly as the champion of the actual occupant. The controversy developed, with varying degrees of bitterness, into a conflict. Street mass meetings at night were addressed by soap box orators, among whom I was more or less conspicuous. Excitement ran high. The situation was tense, and on several occasions we had difficulty in restraining riotous demonstrations.

[*The town of Tombstone had sprung up in a haphazard manner, and in the first years of its existence people bought, improved, and sold property before clear title to the site was established. Adding to the turmoil, the principal officers of the Tombstone Townsite Company, James Clark and Michael Gray, appear to have been unfairly manipulating the situation for their own benefit. (The Townsite Company came into being in 1879 when a group of entrepreneurs filed a "townsite claim" in accordance with the laws governing the private appropriation public domain lands. The townsite overlapped mining claims, causing much confusion about who controlled the surface rights to the property.) The dispute over ownership of Tombstone town lots was complex and it festered in the courts for years. The question became largely moot in the mid 1880s when the mines failed, people left town in droves, and property values plummeted.[16]*]

Barring the [*ownership of lots*] controversy, the general deportment of the citizens of Tombstone during this period was as orderly and decorous as was compatible with a bustling mining camp, and the amenities of social life were observed in a manner

These photos show the rapid growth of Tombstone. The upper image was recorded in the spring of 1880 by Carleton Watkins. The lower photo dates from about 1882 and was taken by C. S. Fly. The Cochise County Courthouse, completed in 1882, can be seen at the far right in the lower picture. Arizona Historical Society, Tucson, #14837 and #26793.

that would compare favorably with similar communities, East or West. Schools were established and somehow I was presented with another job, as chairman of the board of trustees. Two churches were built, Methodist and Episcopal, and the construction of Schieffelin Hall at the corner of Fremont and Fourth streets provided a suitable auditorium for public assemblies. [*Financed by Al Schieffelin, Ed's brother, Schieffelin Hall was completed in June 1881. The two-story adobe opera house became a focal point for Tombstone's cultural life.*[17]]

I was among those active in the organization of the "Tombstone Amateur Dramatic Club" [*founded in the summer of 1881*[18]]. A clipping in an ancient scrapbook relates that we presented "The Toodles" [*on April 9, 1885*[19]]. Mrs. Carrie Gregory impersonated Mrs. Toodles, A. [*Alexander*] J. Mitchell represented Mr. Toodles, while I appeared as Charlie Fenton. Other members of the cast were Miss Bertha Hartman, C. [*Charles*] W. Goodale, Frank Earle, my brother C. [*Cornelius*] W. Clum, and Doctor G. [*George*] C. Willis—all names familiar to the Tombstone public at that time. The clipping concludes with the statement that "The play netted about $120, which is quite an addition to the cemetery fund."

[*Cornelius W. "Casey" Clum (1860-1935) lived in Tombstone for several years. Exactly when he came to Tombstone isn't known, but he was in town as early as February 1882.*[20] *In 1884 the Cochise County Great Register listed Clum as a deputy clerk of the district court. On October 20, 1886, Casey Clum married Mamie (Mary Greer) Herring, daughter of Tombstone attorney and Earp partisan William Herring.*[21] *The Clums moved to Kensington, Maryland, in 1896, where Casey ran a small newspaper,* The Montgomery Press. *He and his wife lived in Maryland for the rest of their lives.*[22]]

The amateur talent of Tombstone produced opera as well as drama, and the rendition of "Pinafore" [*on May 10, 1882*[23]] by our local troupe was fully equal to any professional performance I have ever witnessed. Fred Emerson Brooks was "The Admiral," and Miss Annie Brown was "Little Buttercup." None ever sang these respective parts more effectively. After leaving Tombstone Miss Brown studied music in Europe and then toured the United States with an English opera company. My modest part in the presentation was as a member of the chorus of "Jolly Jack Tars" [*sailors*]. The performance was repeated several times. Social life in Tombstone was on a par with that prevailing in communities of similar size elsewhere, even in the effete East.

As soon as the hectic rush incident to the birth of the "Epitaph" was over, I removed my family from Tucson to Tombstone and purchased two lots on the south side of Safford Street [*between Seventh and Eighth streets24*]. They commanded an enchanting view of that grand sweep of mesas, rolling hills, and mountain ranges stretching away to the west, north, and east, including the famed "Cochise Stronghold" in the Dragoons. On this site I constructed a modest frame cottage and my family was comfortably installed therein about midsummer. This was the second time I had built for them in Arizona. With the approach of the Yuletide season, there was unfeigned joy in our little home when a daughter was born. And then, only a week later, I encountered the major tragedy of my life when, on December 18 [*1880*], my wife passed away. Her remains rest in the old pioneer cemetery at Tombstone [*now known as "Boot Hill"*], and, as if to emphasize the tragic ending of her young life, the ruthless elements during the passing years have swept away every marker from her grave.

[*George Parsons, a young bachelor who had come to Tombstone from California in 1880 to seek his fortune in mining, kept a diary for most of his life. He became a friend of the Clums and on December 18, 1880, he wrote the following in his journal: "Mrs. Clum died this afternoon about five o'clock. Very, very sad. Half of the present female population or more could be better spared than she." December 19: "Mrs. Clum's funeral at three P.M. today . . . . Poor Clum felt his loss severely, but the poor Mother's grief was heartrending. Large funeral."25 Mary "Mollie" Clum, born in Cincinnati on January 18, 1853, was twenty-seven years old at the time of her death. Mollie's widowed mother, (Mary) Angelina Ware, had come to Tombstone shortly before the baby was due.*

In April 1881 John Clum and his mother-in-law took his infant daughter, Bessie (Elizabeth), and two-year-old Woodworth to Washington, D.C.26 There they lived with their paternal grandparents, who had moved to that city. Angelina Ware also resided in Washington and she did her part to care for the grandchildren.27 Little Bessie Clum died on July 7, 1881.28 Woodworth ("Woodie") was raised by his grandparents and two maiden aunts, Jane and Cornelia Clum, and was educated at boarding schools. John Clum visited his son often and later they kept in close touch by letter. Woodworth, like his father, became a newspaperman and local booster, working in Washington, D.C., various towns in Iowa, and Los Angeles.29]

George W. Parsons (1850-1933). The diaries Parsons kept are an invaluable resource for Tombstone researchers. C. S. Fly photo, Arizona Historical Society, Tucson, #1933.

Intense interest was manifested in the approaching city election. Party lines were obliterated. The vital issue was the question of title to city lots—the citizen occupant versus the Townsite Company. [*Clum's own investment in two city lots was threatened by the Townsite Company's claims, so he had more than a passing interest in this dispute.*] The election was held January 4, 1881. Robert Eccleston and Mark P. Shaffer had been nominated as candidates for the office of mayor. Less than a week before the election, Eccleston withdrew and my name was substituted [*by a committee headed by George Parsons[30]*]. The votes totaled 697, of which Shaffer received 165 votes. I received the rest, 532 votes, and thus became the first mayor of [*the "City" of*] Tombstone. Councilmen elected were George A. Pridham, J. [*Julius*] A. Kelly, Godfrey Tribolet, and Smith Gray. These were all candidates on the "Citizens' Protective Ticket," the slogan of which was "Law and order and opposition to the claims of the Townsite Company." This ticket met with opposition from the gambling and saloon element, but was strongly supported by the miners. The first meeting of the council was held January 12, 1881.

[*The January 5, 1881,* Epitaph *reported that incumbent Ben Sippy defeated Howard Lee in the race for city marshal: Sippy 556 votes, Lee 125. In the* Epitaph *article, presumably written by Clum, Lee was described as a pawn of the odious Townsite Company. "The Townsite proprietors get a black eye," the author crowed. Sippy's victory completed the sweep of the election by Clum and his political allies. The opposing faction only mustered one candidate for councilman, Robert Archer, and he was soundly defeated.[31] The election of the "Citizens' Protective" candidates didn't solve the ownership of town lots problem, but the power of the Townsite Company was greatly reduced and the dispute, for the most part, moved from the streets to the courts.*

Besides creating Cochise County, Arizona's eleventh territorial legislature passed a bill incorporating Tombstone as a "city." The measure took effect February 21, 1881.[32] Thus Clum was the first man to serve as mayor under Tombstone's new "city" status. However, the first election to select a mayor and council for the "village" of Tombstone was held on November 24, 1879.[33] When the ballots were counted William A. Harwood emerged as mayor. In compliance with a rule stipulating that municipal elections were to be held the first Tuesday of January, another election took place on January 6, 1880. Alder Randall received the most votes for mayor in this contest.[34] John Clum succeeded Randall in January 1881.]

<> <> <> <> <>

The squeaky old Benson stage [*owned and operated by J. D. Kinnear & Company*] pulled out of Tombstone in the early afternoon of March 15th, 1881, carrying nine passengers and $80,000 in silver bullion. [*Benson, twenty-five miles to the northwest, was the station on the Southern Pacific Railroad closest to Tombstone.*] Fifteen miles out . . . cloudless sky . . . Bud Philpot crooning a desert lullaby from the driver's seat . . . everybody happy . . . sun casting long shadows from the sujuaros [*saguaro cacti, none of which are found between Tombstone and Benson*] . . . . Three men, well masked, emerged from behind a mesquite bush. "Stick 'em up!" or words to that effect. Bob Paul, shotgun messenger [*Wells-Fargo security guard*] sitting alongside the driver, emptied both barrels at the highwaymen. No damage, evidently. A six-gun belched from the road ahead and Bud Philpot tumbled off the driver's seat, dead but still gripping the reins. Then a fusillade. The horses, driverless, stampeded across the desert, the highwaymen following and emptying their guns. Pete Roerig, respectable and peaceful citizen of Tombstone, rolled off the back seat of the stage into the dust. He was dead with a bullet hole through his back. Two, three miles the horses ran before Paul could get hold of the reins. Then back to the roadway and to Benson. Two dead but the bullion safe. [*It is likely that the amount of silver aboard the stage was less than Clum stated. At $1 per ounce, the approximate value of the metal at that time, $80,000 worth would have weighed 5,000 pounds—quite a load for a passenger coach. George Parsons recorded in his diary that the value of the silver on the stage was $26,000.*[35]]

Sheriff Johnny Behan formed a posse of five members and three of them were Earps—Virgil, Wyatt, and Morgan. That showed what the sheriff thought of the Earps in '81. It was a long trek, seventeen days, and in vain. Enemies of the Earps, mostly outlaws and shady gamblers, started grapevine gossip that the three highwaymen were Doc Holliday and two of the Earps. The feud was developing. Doc announced he would make a sieve out of the next low-down blankety-blank who repeated the gossip. Things quieted down—talebearing became a lost art. Months later, Bill Leonard was killed over in New Mexico. As he was passing out, he confessed that he, Jim Crane, and Harry Head had done the Benson stage job. Crane and Head were killed about the same time in six-shooter arguments, but not in Tombstone.

[*Leonard and Head were killed by the Haslett brothers in southwestern New Mexico in June 1881; Crane was killed in the same general area the following August. There are no contemporary documents verifying Clum's statement about Leonard's dying confession. Many scenarios have found their way into print regarding the pursuit of the road agents and subsequent events triggered by the attack on the Benson stage. Rumors ran*

Robert Paul (1830-1901) worked for Wells, Fargo & Company before he became Pima County sheriff in April 1881. Initial results of the November 2, 1880, election gave incumbent sheriff Charles Shibell (a Democrat) a slim lead over Paul (a Republican). Bob Paul challenged the count and the following April the courts declared him the winner. Arizona Historical Society, Tucson, #1596.

rampant and tensions ran high. Different individuals, with different axes to grind, told different stories about what happened and who might have been involved.[36]]

Fred White was our first town marshal in Tombstone. [*White became marshal in November 1879[37] and was elected to a full one-year term as marshal in January 1880.[38]*] His career was cut short by Curly Bill [*Brocius*], an outlaw of parts, whose colorful deeds and misdeeds enliven the pages of Southwest history. Marshal White had informed all the quick-trigger men that there would be no gun toting or six-shooting in Tombstone. If they must shoot out the lights they would have to perform elsewhere—at Galeyville or Charleston—anywhere but Tombstone. But nobody could tell Curly Bill what to do or what not to do—at least so Curly said.

One afternoon [*on October 27, 1880*] Curly and his gang of rustlers drifted into town, imbibed their quota of Arizona whiskey, dropped some spare change at the faro tables, and longed for more excitement. Marshal White walked into the bar to have a look around. Curly and his gang walked out, unlimbered their six-shooters, and took a potshot at Venus or the moon or something. The marshal came running. "What's the big idea?" he asked of Curly Bill. Curly said there wasn't any idea as far as he knew, just boys feelin' good. "Well, I'll take your guns," said Marshal White, "and I'll start with yours first, Curly." Curly pulled out his six-shooter, but just what he really intended to do with it has never been determined.

Wyatt Earp had heard the fusillade and naturally came to see what it was all about. [*Wyatt was a deputy Pima County sheriff— he resigned as deputy about two weeks later.*] He was walking up behind Curly just as Curly pulled his gun. Wyatt, of course, thought Curly was up to some trick, particularly the old "reverse"—handing out the gun, butt towards the other fellow and forefinger inside the trigger-guard. Just as the other fellow is about to grab the gun by the handle, it is swung on the finger and the barrel-end yawns in the other fellow's face instead of the handle. A little pressure with the trigger-finger . . . final curtain for the other fellow. Curly was good at this trick and Wyatt knew it. So he leaped on Curly's back and pinioned Curly's arms to his side. In the melee, Curly's gun was discharged and Marshal White was dead. Wyatt cracked Curly over the head with the butt of his own six-gun and locked Curly up in the town jail. Within fifteen minutes, 500 citizens gathered in front of the jail and demanded Curly for lynching purposes. But Wyatt, six-shooter in hand, told them the law would take its course. It did and Curly was acquitted. He hooked up with the Clantons and the McLowerys and swore death to all the Earps.

[*The fracas during which Marshal White was shot took place shortly after midnight on October 28, 1880.[39] Fred White died on October 30[40] and his funeral was held the next day.[41] The shooting was ruled unintentional, and Curly Bill eventually was*

released from custody without trial.[42] *On October 28, after
learning of Marshal White's injury, the town council appointed
Virgil Earp "assistant marshal" to fill in for him. On November 1,
two days after White's death, the council resolved to hold a
special election on November 12, 1880, for the purpose of
choosing White's replacement. The election was held and Ben
Sippy defeated Virgil Earp, receiving 311 votes to Earp's 259.*[43]
*On January 4, 1881, Tombstone electors voted to retain Sippy as
the town's chief lawman. Many writers have declared that Virgil
Earp lost a second time to Sippy in this election.*[44] *Actually, Virgil
didn't run for town marshal in January 1881. Howard Lee was
Ben's unsuccessful opponent on this occasion.*[45]]

The latter part of April [*1881*] I left Tombstone for a trip to the
states. [*Traveling with Clum were his mother-in-law and his two
young children. They would remain in Washington.*[46]] Among
other things, I was authorized to purchase a fire engine for our fast
growing city, one of those famed old man-power engines. On the
train returning, just east of Benson, we saw a great column of
smoke rising over the hills to the south. I tried to make my fellow
passengers believe we had a live volcano over there, but when I
arrived at Benson I learned that Tombstone was burning. This was
our first big fire and a disastrous one. [*On June 22, 1881, much of
Tombstone's business district burned to the ground.*[47]]

During my absence, Ben Sippy, the city marshal, had
decamped, leaving the city without a police head. Virgil Earp,
with the approval of the city councilmen, had assumed that
responsibility in the emergency and had rendered most efficient
and satisfactory service. I immediately appointed Virgil Earp as
chief of police.

[*Tombstone was incorporated as a "city" on February 21,
1881, and in accordance with the new charter the mayor and
council began drafting an array of ordinances aimed at upgrading
the town's bureaucracy. In April 1881 the Common Council
passed an ordinance which reorganized the marshal's office into
a police department headed by a "chief of police."*[48]]

*On June 6, 1881, the council, with George Pridham presiding
as acting mayor, granted Police Chief Sippy a two-week leave of
absence and appointed Virgil Earp to take over until Sippy got
back from a trip. Sippy didn't return to town when expected and
no one knew his whereabouts. Rumors circulated that he had left*

Tombstone to avoid paying debts. On June 28 Mayor Clum and the council appointed Virgil Earp permanent chief of police by unanimous vote.[49] *Sippy was never seen in Arizona again.*]

In September '81 [*September 8*] Frank Stilwell and Pete Spence [*Spencer?*] robbed the Bisbee stage. Wyatt and Morgan Earp arrested them. Stilwell and Spence were of the Clanton gang of cattle thieves. More nourishment for the showdown that had to come between the laws and the outlaws.

[*According to an article in the September 13, 1881,* Epitaph, *a posse that included Wyatt and Morgan Earp, Deputy Sheriff Billy Breakenridge, and Wells-Fargo agent Marshall Williams arrested Stilwell (himself a deputy Cochise County sheriff) and Spence in Bisbee, believing them to be the stage robbers.*[50] *Neither of the accused men was convicted of the crime.*]

3

GERONIMO BREAKS LOOSE

Instead of hanging Geronimo in 1877, the army removed the shackles, forgave him his murders and robberies, told him to be a good Indian, and turned him loose. The army folks had a weird psychology in those days. They put irons on Eskiminzin (always a good Indian) because he was an Apache and some major did not like him; they took the irons off of Geronimo (always a bad Indian) because they wanted to show the Apaches that the army occasionally could be magnanimous. The effect, however, was to disgust and dishearten the good Apaches and embolden the former renegades.

Geronimo remained at San Carlos many months after the army restored his freedom, receiving free food and free blankets from our government, fraternizing with army officers, and, incidently, developing his organization for robbing and killing more White men. Geronimo was very smart or our army officers were very dumb or both.

In [*August*] 1878,[1] about a year after I had captured him, Geronimo quietly slipped out of the San Carlos Reservation and went to Mexico. For a year he remained beyond Uncle Sam's jurisdiction, committed a few depredations just to keep in practice, and further developed his renegade organization. In the fall of 1879 he returned to San Carlos, where he again received government food, government blankets, and official sympathy. [*Geronimo surrendered to U.S. troops in December 1879 and arrived at San Carlos in January 1880.[2]*] He carried on a constant propaganda amongst the Apaches at the reservation, claiming that White soldiers had given him his freedom because they were afraid of him, and spreading more of that buncombe [*bunk*] about his charmed life as the favored son of Usen [*an Apache deity*]. [*Geronimo was a "medicine man" and his followers believed that he had supernatural powers—was clairvoyant, impervious to bullets, etc.[3]*]

During the night of September 29th [*October 1[4]*], 1881, red men moved quietly amongst the wooded canyons of the San Carlos Reservation. The high sign was given, the password spoken. With the coming of the dawn, Geronimo and five hundred Apaches, including Nah-chee [*Naiche*] (son of Cochise), had fled. The tragic Geronimo campaign had begun. A pall of terror spread

Chiricahua Apaches in northern Sonora. Left to right, Perico, Geronimo, Naiche, Tsisnah. Photo taken in March 1886 by C. S. Fly. Arizona Historical Society, Tucson, #78163.

over the White population of Arizona. [*Between three and four hundred Chiricahua Apaches bolted the reservation in this outbreak. Fewer than one hundred were warriors, the rest women and children.*5]

Two days later, October 2nd [*5th* 6], 1881, I was sitting in my office in Tombstone, trying to hold down my job as mayor. A courier rushed in and reported that Geronimo and his gang were on the warpath and had been seen less than an hour before near the Dragoon Mountains, ten miles from [*northeast of*] Tombstone, headed toward Mexico. The courier had spread his news as he galloped down Tombstone's main street. "Indians are coming!" had been an American frontier call-to-arms for two hundred years; in Arizona, "Geronimo is coming!" sent women to dark corners and brought vigilantes running, guns in hand, ready to go. Of course, Tombstone, with its 10,000 [*5,000*] population, was in no danger from Geronimo and 500 renegades, but we feared for the safety of isolated cattlemen in the Sulphur Springs Valley, as well as for solitary prospectors, overland stage passengers, and others who might be in the mountains or along the trails.

In view of my former experience with the Apaches and the further fact that I was then mayor of Tombstone, I was charged with the organization of a company of horsemen for the purpose of following the trail of the renegades. Our chief object was to give assistance to anyone who might be in need of it. Beyond that, our actions would be governed entirely by developments. The number of saddle horses immediately available was limited, and it was important that these should be assigned to the right sort of men. These men must be equipped with rifles, six-shooters, ammunition, saddlebags, and canteens. Equally important was the matter of rations. Every moment occupied with the details put the renegades just that much further ahead of us. The men selected for the trip were impatient for the start, and this impatience grew as the first hour passed, and the second, and still the third, until at one o'clock in the afternoon all preparations were complete and our little cavalcade of 35 experienced frontiersmen galloped up Allen Street and took the trail for Antelope Pass [*east of town*].

In those good old days, Tombstone did not lack for men with well established reputations for being handy with a gun. There were in this company Virgil Earp (my chief of police) and his two brothers Wyatt and Morgan, Johnny Behan and W. [*William*] M. Breakenridge of the sheriff's office, Charlie Reppy, Frank Ingoldsby, George W. Parsons, Ward Priest, Marshall Williams, Cy [*Silas H.*] Bryant, and others who had been weighed in the balance and not found wanting.

Arizona is renowned as an arid country, but there are occasional downpours, which, for quantity of dampness, are unexcelled anywhere in the world. It was our luck to encounter such a storm in Antelope Pass. We had just struck the fresh trail left by Geronimo and his renegades and had quickened our pace in the hope of closing up with them by nightfall, or at least surprising them before they broke camp the next morning, when rain began falling in torrents. Heavy thunder was continuous, and vivid lightning was sporting among the rocks all about us. Soon everyone was wet, and, although the thunder and lightning ceased as we descended from the pass, the rain persisted until nearly midnight.

Just as we reached the western rim of Sulphur Springs Valley we found four companies of cavalry in camp on the trail. These had come down the valley from the railroad, thinking that the renegades might cross to that side of the Dragoon range. But as soon as they had struck the hot trail they promptly made camp. When we inquired the reason for this untimely halt, we were told that it was "too wet to travel." As a matter of fact, traveling in rain and mud was no holiday pastime. Our clothing was soaked through to the skin, our boots full of water, and the soft ground was very tiring to our horses, although we could go no faster than a walk. But with the average frontiersman it is never too wet to travel unless he is actually stuck in the mud. Furthermore, we did not know who, even then, might be lying wounded and suffering. We bid the soldiers good night and trudged on down the valley.

It was nearly midnight when we reached a small shack on one of the cattle ranges. Rain had ceased, clouds were breaking. The moon would rise about two o'clock in the morning, and, as we had been riding since one o'clock that afternoon, we decided to give our horses a rest and wait for the moon. We picketed our horses and set a guard, started a fire in the shack, and made ourselves as comfortable as circumstances would permit, meanwhile munching hardtack or whatever other edible was found in the saddlebags. There was bantering as to whose clothes were wettest, whose boots held the most water. It was well we all had a sense of humor because the 35 of us could not get into the shack at the same time unless all of us were standing. S.R.O. [*standing room only*] and no sleep.

At 2 a.m. the moon peered over the eastern horizon—time for us to resume our march. In silence each one sought his horse—no orders were necessary. It hurt to sit again upon those sore spots aggravated by wet saddles and wetter clothes. But none uttered the slightest protest. We were after Geronimo. Cinches were adjusted, men swung into saddles, and, aided by the bright moonlight, we moved along the soggy trail. The march continued in silence until daylight, for we were tired and sleepy. But with the breaking of day, our spirits revived.

At noon we knew we had crossed the international line and were trespassing in Mexico. Evidently the hostiles had not found it too wet to travel. Fortunately, they had not met either man or beast on their stampede down the valley; at least nothing had been killed by them along the trail. We had accomplished the purpose of our undertaking, and we had no right to invade Mexico. Furthermore, we were not equipped for an indefinite campaign. We were out of grub and hungry. Before leaving Tombstone we had arranged to have a man follow us with a buckboard loaded with provisions. Doubtless he had started, but, like the army, had found it too wet to travel with a loaded wagon. For an hour we speculated as to how far we were in Mexico, how far the renegades were ahead of us, how far we would have to ride on the back trail before we would meet the chuckwagon. The more we discussed the contents of that chuckwagon, the keener became the pangs of hunger. Without a dissenting voice, we headed our horses northward toward the U.S.A. and Tombstone.

It was nearly sundown when we again met the soldiers—in the same camp where we had left them twenty-four hours before. There was no necessity for them to go further southward now, for the trail of the renegades was not only wet but likewise very cold. Geronimo and his followers no longer had to fear pursuit by American troops. Near by the military camp we spied our delayed buckboard with its precious cargo. Having satisfied our hunger and puffed a cigarette or two, we rolled up in our blankets, slept soundly and long.

Up with the dawn, we saddled our horses and were off in a bunch for Tombstone, leaving the troops still camping on the trail of the renegades. We headed for Antelope Pass. Our strenuous march had not been rewarded by a single stirring adventure. The ample supper and breakfast, and intervening sleep, had fully refreshed our party. We were all in fine fettle. This exuberance of spirits manifested itself in various stunts, which included cowboy tricks, fancy riding, and target shooting. Expert riders in our party demonstrated the proper method of fighting Indians on the plains: urging their mounts to full speed and then, leaning far to one side, clinging with the left arm over the horse's shoulder, they discharged their six-shooters underneath his neck.

As leader, I maintained the dignity of the party and contented myself with witnessing the successive feats and heartily applauding the actors. But I was jarred loose from my passive attitude when the company halted suddenly and demanded that I assassinate a prairie dog that was periscoping with his head just above the mound which encircled the entrance to his subterranean abode. These men had never seen me shoot, nor had they ever heard me boast of my prowess as a dead shot. As a matter of fact, I was never too confident of my ability to hit the bull's eye, but I realized that my reputation with these men was now at stake. I halted my horse, and, without dismounting, slipped my rifle from its sling, straightened myself in the saddle, drew a bead on the prairie dog, and fired. With the crack of the gun the prairie dog disappeared in his hole. None went to see whether or not the little animal had been hit. That was not necessary, for the bullet had plowed its way through both edges of the circular mound on a direct line with the former position of the prairie dog's head. I had scored the perfect shot. Without batting an eye or seeming the least surprised, I slipped my rifle back into its sling and moved forward on the trail.

My audience expressed approval, but all were not convinced. We had ridden less than a mile when a hawk was seen perched on the summit of the stalk of a century plant. Instantly there was unanimous demand for "another shot by the mayor." When I attempted to make the second shot from the saddle, my horse refused to stand still. So I dismounted, took aim, and fired. This time there was nothing to mark the track of the bullet, and as the hawk spread its wings and left its perch I felt chagrined. The hawk started a graceful circle upward, but had moved less than ten feet when a single feather was seen fluttering towards the ground. My spirits rose, for, at least, my bullet had cut into the plumage of the target. The hawk continued its upward flight for an additional ten or fifteen feet, then dropped to the ground like a plummet. Everybody was convinced, except me, and my skill with the rifle was never again questioned. Luckily.

[*Geronimo remained on the loose in Mexico, occasionally raiding into Arizona, until February 1884. He then surrendered and returned to the San Carlos Reservation, only to go on the warpath again in 1885. Geronimo and his band surrendered to the U.S. Army for the last time in 1886 and subsequently were exiled to Florida. The Chiricahuas were transferred to Alabama in 1887 and were sent to Oklahoma in 1894. Geronimo died in Oklahoma in 1909. He was in his eighties at the time of his death.*[7]]

4

THE EARP-CLANTON BATTLE

The Geronimo scare had been forgotten. Three weeks had passed since our posse returned from its unsuccessful chase of the renegades. Life in Tombstone had resumed normalcy, business was at the peak of prosperity, and the crisp, clear air of late October put us all in good spirits.

There was a very dangerous element at that time in the country adjacent to Tombstone, more or less nomadic, and including stage robbers, cattle rustlers, and other desperadoes. So serious was this that we organized a "Citizens' Safety Committee" of two hundred representative business and professional men of the city for the purpose of supporting duly authorized officers of the law in maintaining order within the city limits and protecting the lives and property of citizens, particularly in the event of an invasion by the lawless outside element. As mayor, I was the head of this committee.

[*The activities of Clum's vigilance committee appear to have been mostly political. There is no record of Clum and his businessman friends stringing up an outlaw, as vigilantes occasionally did elsewhere. A mob of angry miners from Bisbee, not Tombstone people, hung John Heath in 1884.[1] This was the only lynching to take place in Tombstone.[2] Also, the notion that an "invasion" of Tombstone by an army of desperadoes was a possibility seems farfetched. Earlier in his memoir Clum himself indicated that only a handful of men (the Clantons, McLaurys, and their friends) were responsible for most of the lawlessness in the vicinity—hardly an invasion force.*]

News was scarce for my next issue of "The Epitaph," so [*on the morning of October 26, 1881*] I wandered up-town in search for a human-interest story. Ike Clanton was leaning against an adobe wall at the corner of Fremont and Fourth streets holding a Winchester rifle in his arms much after the fashion of a mother holding her child, and fondling it accordingly. The Clanton family had lived in the Gila valley, not far from the eastern boundary of the Indian reservation, during the time I was in charge of the Apaches at San Carlos. I formed a casual acquaintance with several members of the Clanton clan at that time and had been on speaking terms with Ike ever since. In '79 the Clantons moved to a ranch west from Tombstone in the San Pedro valley and made it

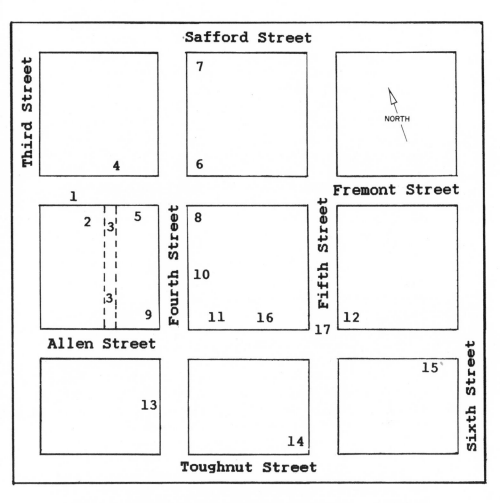

Downtown Tombstone circa 1881-1882. Key: 1. Approximate site of the Earp-Holliday/Clanton-McLaury shootout. 2. C. S. Fly's boarding house and photo gallery. 3. O.K. Corral (the corral/livery stable had entrances on both Fremont and Allen streets.) 4. Tombstone Epitaph *office. 5.* Tombstone Nugget *office. 6. Schieffelin Hall. 7. Turn Verein Hall. 8. Post office. 9. Can-Can Restaurant. 10. Spangenberg's Gun Shop. 11. Cosmopolitan Hotel 12. Oriental Saloon. 13. Justice of the Peace A. O. Wallace's courtroom. 14. Russ House (hotel and restaurant). 15. Bird Cage Theatre. 16. Campbell & Hatch's Billiard Parlor (where Morgan Earp was assassinated). 17. Virgil Earp was here when he was shot from ambush.*

headquarters for outlaws in that section, a clearinghouse for cattle
stolen in Mexico by the rustlers and smuggled across the line.
[*The Clanton place was a few miles south of Charleston.*] Ike had
been warned to keep out of Tombstone, and it was against the
town law to carry firearms. [*Clum implies that Ike Clanton had
been told to stay out of town by the chief of police or someone else
in authority, but convincing evidence that such a warning had
been issued is lacking. However, the common council indeed had
passed an ordinance that prohibited the carrying of deadly
weapons in Tombstone without a special permit.*[3]] My nose for
news told me there was a good story in the making, my conscience as mayor told me that Ike should be arrested and my story
ruined.

"Good morning, Ike," I said. "Any new war on today?"

"Nothin' perticular," drawled Ike, turning on his cowboy heel
and ambling down Fourth Street. That convinced me that Ike had
something sinister on his mind, because usually he was more
talkative, less taciturn. While I was debating what to do, I saw our
chief of police, Virgil Earp, sauntering down the street toward Ike.

"Hello, Ike," said Virgil. "What are you doing in town?"

"Nothin' perticular," replied Ike.

"Why the Winchester?"

"Oh, just happened to have it with me," said Ike, edging away.

"Wait a minute, Ike," said Virgil, taking hold of Ike's arm.
"Let's you and I go over and call on Judge Wallace. You can tell
him why you brought that cannon in town with you." All of which
meant, of course, that Ike was arrested.

They walked down the street, Virgil still holding Ike's arm.
Suddenly Ike made a break, tried to wrench away from Virgil's
grip. But Virgil was on the job, pulled his six-shooter, and cracked
Ike over the head with the butt end of it. Ike stretched his length
on the sidewalk. Wyatt and Morgan Earp happened along about
that time. The Earp brothers had an uncanny habit of happening
along when trouble was brewing. Virgil, Wyatt, and Morgan
disarmed Ike, revived him, and took him to the court where Judge
[*Albert O.*] Wallace fined him $25 and retained his weapons.

Ike did not like that a bit. "Wait till I get another gun," he
yelled. "I'll kill every damn one of you Earps." Whereupon
Morgan Earp pulled his own six-shooter out of its holster and
offered it to Ike, handle first. Ike tried to grab it, but one of the
deputy sheriffs pushed Ike back and told Morgan to put his gun
away and get out of the court room. The three Earps walked out
together, Ike tagging on behind still raving about how he was

going to kill all of the Earps on sight.

Standing just outside the doorway was Tom McLowery, one of Ike Clanton's buddies and as tough an outlaw as was raised in those parts. A mean looking six-gun was sticking out from Tom's belt. "You Earps are a lot of ---- -- ------s," swore Tom. "I'll shoot it out with you anytime, anywhere."

"All right, Tom," said Wyatt Earp, "now's a good time and this is a good place, right here in front of the courtroom." As Wyatt spoke he slapped McLowery's face with his left hand and pulled his six-gun with his right hand. McLowery made no move. Cowardice makes a brave man mad. Wyatt flared up. "Pull your gun and fight, you yellow-livered skunk," roared Wyatt, "or I'll break this six-shooter over your head." Still McLowery made no move. That was the last straw. Down came Wyatt's gun on Tom's head and Tom passed out, temporarily. The three Earps walked down the street. [*Wyatt Earp later testified that Tom McLaury was armed when he met him outside the courtroom, but some doubt that this was true. If Tom had a "mean looking six-gun" in his belt, why didn't the Earps arrest him for carrying a firearm in town? They arrested Ike Clanton for this reason, so why not Tom McLaury?[4]*]

Busy forenoon, much conversation, but not a shot fired. I hurried back to the "Epitaph" office to write the story. It was a rattling good story, too, because for over a year the Clanton-McLowery gang of outlaws had been threatening to clean up Tombstone and the Earps. Virgil Earp was chief of police and a good one; Wyatt Earp was marshal. So the Earps represented the law and I was back of them 100 percent, both as mayor and as editor. Enforcing the law in Tombstone in 1880 and 1881 was not child's play; it was serious work for he-men.

[*Besides being Tombstone's chief of police, Virgil Earp, not Wyatt, was a deputy U.S. marshal. However, Virgil later testified before Judge Wells Spicer that he had deputized both Wyatt and Morgan Earp as "special" policemen several weeks prior to the fateful day of October 26, 1881.[5] Frontier lawmen, lacking adequate staffs of full-time officers, often deputized trusted townspeople with law enforcement experience to help them in emergencies. These part-time, special deputies usually were not carried on official rosters of city or county employees and were paid only after services were rendered.[6]*]

Ike Clanton picked Tom McLowery up out of the gutter. Billy Clanton and Frank McLowery had been consuming a little liquor at the Oriental. They heard the news and went to the help of their

Chief of Police Virgil Earp (1843-1905, upper left) and his "special" deputies: upper right, Wyatt Earp (1848-1929); lower left, Morgan Earp (1851-1882); lower right, John H. "Doc" Holliday (1851-1887). Arizona Historical Society, Tucson, #1444, #1447, #1442, and #1502.

respective brothers. Billy [*William F.*] Claiborne, buddy of the Clantons, went along. All five went to the gunsmith's, evidently to add to their arsenal and ammunition supply. Then they repaired to the O.K. Corral for further conference. The O.K. Corral was on Fremont Street, directly opposite the office of the "Epitaph." But I was busy with my story and did not notice them.

The McLowery brothers had a ranch about 25 miles east from Tombstone in the Sulphur Springs Valley, where they harbored and fed the cattle thieves and other desperadoes of that locality and looked after the interests of those rustlers who imported their stolen stock by way of Agua Prieta [*a Sonoran border town near present-day Douglas, Arizona*]. The McLowery ranch was a rendezvous for as tough an assortment of cattle thieves, stage robbers, murderers, and all-around crooks as ever assembled on any frontier.

When the three Earps walked away from the prostrate form of Tom McLowery, they were joined by Doc Holliday and went into the Can-Can [*Restaurant*] for lunch. About half past two there was a commotion in the O.K. Corral. Sheriff Behan was having an argument with the five members of the Clanton-McLowery gang. Somebody had told the Earps that the Clanton-McLowerys were organizing for a fight to the death. The Earps, always obliging in such matters, were on their way to the O.K. Corral to see about it. The sheriff had tried to disarm and arrest the Clanton gang but had failed both ways. He then went to intercept the Earps. But the Earps pushed him to one side and came marching on, Virgil and Wyatt in front, Morgan and Doc Holliday behind. Sheriff Behan brought up the rear, demanding peace in the name of the law.

The Clanton crowd was huddled close to the gate of the corral. The Earps walked up to within five feet of the Clantons. [*The confrontation took place on the south side of Fremont Street a few doors west of the corral. The men were not far from the* Epitaph *office, but Clum did not observe the showdown.*] "Ike," said Virgil, "there has been a lot of loose talk around town by you and your gang of cutthroats. Throw up your hands, all of you!" The answer came instantly from two six-shooters. Then more six-shooters blazed so quickly they sounded like echoes of the first. Frank McLowery fell, shot through the abdomen. Tom McLowery ran to his nearby horse to get his rifle. Doc Holliday unlimbered his short-barrel shotgun and literally blew Tom into pieces. Morgan Earp drilled a hole clear through Billy Clanton's chest, but the game lad lay crumpled against the wall, calmly pouring lead at his adversaries.

Looking east on Fremont Street about 1882. The Epitaph *office is in the building at the far left, Schieffelin Hall is the tall building with the flag pole. The photographer was standing near the spot where the Earp-Holliday/Clanton-McLaury gunfight took place. Arizona Historical Society, Tucson, #60575.*

Ike Clanton made a leap for Wyatt's gun arm, like that old squaw did to [*Clay*] Beauford when we were arresting Geronimo [*in 1877*], hoping to get Wyatt's gun out of commission. Wyatt could have killed Ike without even hesitating in the general warfare, but Wyatt was not that sort of fighter. He cracked Ike's knuckles with the barrel of his six-shooter, pushed Ike off, told him to run or fight and to be damn quick making up his mind. Ike beat it, to use a very modern expression. After the shooting stopped, Ike was discovered in the dark room of Fly's photograph gallery. So much for Ike.

Virgil Earp was prone on the ground, a bullet from Billy Clanton's gun having gone through his leg. But Virgil was still shooting. He clipped a piece out of Billy Clanton's ten-gallon hat. Billy shifted his position, took a potshot at Morgan Earp, and Morgan fell with a hole in his shoulder. Johnny Behan, the sheriff, ran into the photograph gallery—bullets were flying too thick for Johnny. Frank McLowery, blood streaming from a gaping wound in his stomach, saw Morgan Earp fall. With heroic effort, Frank got to his feet and staggered toward Morgan, gun in hand. "Quick, Morg," yelled Wyatt, "get Frank McLowery!" Doc Holliday heard Wyatt's warning, turned quickly, and fired point blank at the tottering Frank. Morgan let loose at the same moment. Frank dropped in his tracks, dead. It is still a matter of dispute in Tombstone whether Doc or Morgan killed Frank McLowery. The important thing was that Frank was permanently out of the picture. Billy Clanton, with two holes through his middle, lay inert against the adobe wall.

These men bit the dust in the shootout with the Earp party: left, Frank McLaury (1848-1881); right, Tom McLaury (1853-1881). The true character of the McLaury brothers is difficult to determine. Arizona Historical Society, Tucson, #24364 and #24365.

Wyatt Earp, unscathed, looked over the field and reloaded his six-shooter. But the war was over. Of the five members of the Clanton gang, the two McLowerys and Billy Clanton were dead, Ike was hiding in the dark room, and Billy Claiborne had disappeared before the fight started. Virgil and Morgan Earp lay in the middle of Fremont Street, wounded but poised on elbows, guns ready to spit more death should any more of Ike's friends put in an appearance. Doc Holliday stood alongside Wyatt. Somebody's bullet had burned a nice little furrow along Doc's thigh, otherwise he had been untouched. The entire battle had lasted less than half a minute. [*There are many versions of the gunfight, and opinions differ about who shot first and who shot whom. Although*

*he did not witness the event, Clum's reconstruction of the shootout
is probably about as good as any.*]

"Well, Doc," said Wyatt, "guess the show is over. Let's take
Virg and Morg up to the doctor's."

"O. K.," agreed Doc. "They're not badly hurt." [*Virgil's wound
was not life-threatening, but Morgan's was serious.*] And the four
of them started down Fremont Street. Sheriff Behan slipped out of
his hiding place and approached the quartette.

"Wyatt," he said, "I think I will have to arrest you boys for
murder." Wyatt pushed Johnny aside and said nothing. "I say,
Wyatt . . . "

Wyatt stopped, looked at the sheriff with those cold, steel-grey
eyes of his. "Behan," he said, "you had your chance to do some
arresting before the fight. If you had locked up that bunch of cutthroats when they came into town, there'd been no trouble. We
haven't murdered anybody. We've only done our duty to Tombstone and to ourselves. Trot along now and forget it." And Johnny
trotted. But the next day he reappeared and arrested them.

The trial was in November before Judge Spicer. In acquitting
the Earps and Holliday, the judge said it was immaterial who shot
first or who shot whom. The dead men were outlaws, he said,
quick on the trigger, dangerous. If the Earps had not shot first,
they would have been killed themselves and that would have been
a calamity for Tombstone. It was a very sound and fearless
opinion.

[*The proceeding before Justice of the Peace Wells Spicer was
a preliminary hearing, not a full-blown trial. It was held to
determine whether there was sufficient evidence of wrongdoing by
the Earp party to warrant referring the case to a grand jury.[7] The
judge decided that the Earps and Holliday had been justified in
their actions and there was no need for further inquiry into the
matter.[8] In spite of this finding, Virgil Earp, who had been
suspended as chief of police by Mayor Clum and the town council
after the shootout, was not returned to duty. James Flynn had
been appointed as Virgil's replacement, and he remained acting
police chief until the January 1882 municipal election. Throughout 1881 Virgil Earp retained his commission as a deputy U.S.
marshal.[9]*]

Before and during the trial I was strong for the Earps. I
believed in them and have held that opinion for fifty years. I
supported them in the "Epitaph" and denounced the outlaws. The
acquittal of the Earps and Doc Holliday was approved by all of the
good citizens of Tombstone. But Ike Clanton was peeved. He had

The result of the "Gunfight at the O.K. Corral:" Tom McLaury (left), Frank McLaury (center), and nineteen-year-old Billy Clanton in their coffins. After an elaborate funeral, they were buried in the Tombstone cemetery. Arizona Historical Society, Tucson, #17483.

gone back to his ranch and was busy reconstructing his pirate crew. A week or two later, rumors began floating around town that the outlaws planned reprisals and had prepared a list of those who were to be "bumped off" at the first opportunity. My name and Judge Spicer's were said to rank fifth and sixth on the list. [*Others reported to be on the outlaws' hit list were Virgil, Morgan, and Wyatt Earp, Tom Fitch (Wyatt's attorney), Doc Holliday, and Wells-Fargo agent Marshall Williams.*[10]] Of course, we did not believe all we heard in those days, but the situation was tense and I confess I began packing my six-gun around with me, something I never had done before. It's all right to sit in your library in these more civilized days and talk about ignoring rumored threats of that sort; but in Tombstone in '81 conditions were different. I knew the character of the surviving outlaws and did not relish being shot in the back after dark. So I kept my six-shooter handy and my ear to the ground. [*A Colt "single-action army" revolver, caliber .44-40, that once belonged to Clum is now on display in the Gene Autry Western Heritage Museum in Los Angeles.*[11]]

Incidently, I was still postmaster of Tombstone, and three times we picked up rumors that the outlaws were headed for town to rob the post office. Each time I invited two or three friends to spend the night with me sleeping in the post office well healed with guns and ammunition. You may think it took a lot of nerve to invite friends to spend the night with you under such circumstances. But that was the way of the West in those days. However, nothing happened and things about town soon returned to normal.

Too bad that the normal life of a community has no news value—only the abnormal has reader interest. There were lots of good folks living in Tombstone in those days, about whose unselfish deeds whole chapters might, and should, be written. For instance, that remarkable Irish girl Nellie Cashman. There was a "frontiersman" for you! Born in Queenstown, Ireland, [*in 1845*] about the same time I was born in the shadows of the Catskills, she emigrated with her sister in '66, didn't care much for Boston, and arrived in San Francisco in '68. She joined the Cassiar gold rush in '77 in northern British Columbia, was at Virginia City in '78, Tucson in '79, and arrived in Tombstone in '80.

[*Nellie Cashman came to America with her mother and sister about 1850. The family moved from Boston to San Francisco in 1865 or 1866. The year 1872 found Nellie running a boarding house in the mining town of Pioche, Nevada, and by 1874 she was in western Canada. In 1876 she returned to San Francisco; in 1879 Nellie opened a restaurant in Tucson; in 1880 she joined the silver rush to Tombstone and became proprietor of an eatery and hotel.*[12]]

Within a month or so, everybody in town knew Nellie Cashman. She was here, there, and everywhere, doing good all the time. For livelihood, she operated the Russ House, a miners' hotel. For avocation, she was Tombstone's guardian angel. We had no hospital in Tombstone, so Nellie took charge of the sick and injured. Citizens supported her charities generously and without hesitation. If she asked for a contribution, we contributed; if she had tickets to sell, we bought tickets; if she wanted actors for an entertainment, we acted. Nellie was an inspiration in all matters of philanthropy and charity. She associated more with men than with women, tramped trails with them, shared their hardships. But her reputation was unimpeachable, clean, courageous, respected and admired in every community in which she lived. And she lived in many.

Nellie's sister [*Fanny*], back in 1870, had married Thomas Cunningham in San Francisco. In 1880 [*1881*] Mr. Cunningham died, leaving his widow and five children and no funds. Nellie did not even hesitate. She brought the widow and her brood to Tombstone at once and made a comfortable home for them. Three years later [*in 1884*], the mother, Nellie's sister, died, and Nellie brought up the five children as her own, educated them, and gave them all a good start in life.

[*John Clum did not live in Tombstone during 1883 and 1884, and he would have learned about events that took place in those years from others. Much of the following narrative detailing Nellie's Tombstone exploits is not substantiated by contemporary records and is probably folklore.*[13]]

Five men were convicted of murder[*s*] [*committed*] in Bisbee and sentenced to hang in Tombstone, the county seat. Nellie was a devout Catholic, but her ministrations were not restricted to any sect or creed. She visited the condemned men and prayed with them, urged them to make their peace with God. Nellie was not a sob sister. She knew the men deserved hanging and she was all for it. But she wanted to save their souls if she could.

[*In December 1883 the five men in question killed several people during a Bisbee robbery. They were soon caught and lodged in the Tombstone jail. In February 1884 they were tried, convicted, and sentenced to hang. A sixth member of the gang, John Heath, had helped plan the robbery but did not do any shooting. Heath was sentenced to a lengthy term in prison. Disagreeing with such lenient treatment, on February 22, 1884, an enraged mob of miners from Bisbee snatched Heath from the jailhouse and hung him from a telephone pole.*[14]]

Time came for the executions. Some local men were sordid enough to erect a grandstand adjoining the courthouse yard and sold tickets at a dollar apiece to see the hanging. Better citizens were indignant. A protest meeting was held, but no legal remedy was in sight. On the afternoon preceding the executions, Nellie communicated with twenty-five or thirty miners upon whom she knew she could depend. She told them to report at the Russ House at 2 a.m. armed with crowbars and sledgehammers. Of course,

Irate miners from Bisbee lynched John Heath in Tombstone on February 22, 1884. Arizona Historical Society, Tucson, #4937.

they reported. She led them to the grandstand. "Down she comes, boys," said Nellie, "and we'll take most of the lumber away with us, too." Came the dawn [*on March 28, 1884*] and no grandstand. The executions were private, inside the courtyard. [*An article in the March 29, 1884,* Tombstone Republican *noted that five hundred people holding tickets issued by Sheriff Jerome Ward were admitted into the jail yard to witness this hanging.*[15]]

Trouble was brewing in the Grand Central Mine [*in 1884*]. Striking miners in ugly mood proposed to kidnap E. B. Gage, the superintendent, and hang him. Nellie Cashman had always befriended the miners, so it was easy for her to obtain news of the plot. The job was to be pulled at midnight. But at 10 p.m. Nellie and her familiar buggy drove up to the Gage residence on the hill just south of town. "Some of the striking miners are going to kidnap you at midnight and hang you at 1 a.m., or thereabouts," Nellie told Mr. Gage. "I have come to take you for a little buggy ride to Benson where you can catch the train for Tucson." Through the night they drove, and the plot was frustrated. Next day the miners found out who spoiled their party and how. "Guess she's right, at that," they said. "There'd been hell to pay if we'd strung up the boss." And Nellie was more popular than ever. One of God's noblewomen was Nellie Cashman, frontiersman. [*Nellie Cashman left a slumping Tombstone in 1887 and continued her rambling among of the mining camps of the West.[16]*]

Another name overlooked by the "colorful" writers—Fred Emerson Brooks, sometime postmaster at Tombstone, singer, entertainer, poet, and athlete. Fred personated "The Admiral" in that local amateur presentation of "Pinafore," and none ever sang that role more acceptably. On July 4, 1881, I presided at the patriotic exercises held in Schieffelin Hall and introduced Fred Brooks as the poet of the day. Fred read a humorous poem, replete with local hits, which was received with much laughter and applause. This was his initial appearance before the public as a poet, and the pronounced success of that effort was the inspiration that eventually brought him distinction as "The Poet-Humorist of California." Fred Brooks published several volumes of his verses, the first of which was entitled, "Old Ace and Other Poems." His "Pickett's Charge at Gettysburg," an heroic historical poem, is the peer of any similar creation in the English language. Yes, there were many charming and interesting people in Tombstone who never even owned a six-gun.

5

ADIEU TO THE EARPS

One evening a week or so before Christmas '81 [*December 14, 1881*], I climbed into the Benson stage for the first lap of a journey to Washington to spend Yuletide with my parents [*and with three-year-old Woodworth*]. I had kept my going secret—no use spreading the news and inviting my outlaw friends to gather somewhere along the highway. At least, I thought I had kept it secret. Later I discovered I had not.

The stage had gone only three miles from Tombstone, the stars were beautiful and clear, the Huachucas [*Huachuca Mountains*] rugged and sinister in silhouette. From the roadside came shouts of "Halt!" and "Stick 'em up!" Ike and his bad boys evidently did not intend to let me get far from home. Three pistol shots echoed in the night air. I knew enough not to stick my head out through the window to see what was happening. In fact, I knew quite well what was happening and got my six-shooter in position where it would do the most good, or harm, depending upon the point of view. Came a second command to halt. Our driver applied the brakes, very much against my mental protests. Another salvo of shots. That was fortunate. The horses became frightened and lunged forward so furiously that the brakes did not hold. That, in turn, gave Jimmie Harrington, our driver, a wonderful idea. He released the brakes altogether and whipped the horses into a run. More shots from the highwaymen. But we were well on our way and out of range.

For half a mile we bowled along at full gallop. The other four passengers in the stage were huddled on the floor where they had precipitated themselves when the first shot rang out. They yelled at me to drop down or I would be shot. But I had other plans. I had two six-shooters and was thinking fast how I might be able to use them to the best advantage if we were commanded to halt a second time. I reasoned that the outlaws would reload their guns, mount their horses, and make another attempt to stop us further down the road. Realizing that I had small chance for either defense or escape if I remained in the coach, I opened the door and stood with one foot on the step while I watched for trouble ahead. Suddenly the driver applied the brakes, and someone shouted from the road ahead of us. Before the stage had stopped, I was on the ground and beyond the range of the rays of the sidelights [*oil-burning lamps*], both six-shooters ready for action.

But this was a false alarm. "Whistling Dick" [*Dick Wright*], driver of the bullion wagon, had followed us out from Tombstone. He was going down empty and was close behind our coach when the shooting began. Frightened by the shooting, his team broke into a run, and, not having any load, they ran past our coach on the left side (opposite from me) and on down the road before Dick could stop them. It was Dick's voice I had heard from the road ahead of us. Dick said he had been shot in the leg. Jimmie Harrington said his "off leader" [*the lead horse on the left*] was staggering. We found that the leader had been shot through the neck and was bleeding to death. When the coach did not stop on command, the highwaymen had attempted to kill one of our horses. Dick's wound was not serious. We rendered first aid by wrapping a couple of handkerchiefs around his leg, covering the wound. Then we cut the two leaders from the stage team. [*The coach was drawn by six horses in three pairs.[1]*] Jimmie Harrington mounted on the box, straightened out his ribbons [*reins*], and sang out, "All aboard."

A stagecoach of the type in use during the 1880s. Arizona Historical Society, Tucson, #28618.

But I had stepped about fifty paces into the darkness to look and listen for sight or sound of horsemen. As I looked at the coach

with its sidelights, I realized that my presence in the coach only
jeopardized the other passengers. I was much better off with my
feet on the ground and no sidelights. I struck off through the
mesquite and cactus on foot. After a precarious trek, in and out of
ravines, I arrived at the Grand Central quartz mill about one
o'clock a.m. The mill superintendent was a friend and I told him
my story. He telephoned to Tombstone that I was safe. [*The first
telephone systems were being installed in Arizona and, according
to an article in the April 10, 1881,* Arizona Weekly Citizen
(Tucson), *a line had been run between Tombstone and the Grand
Central Mill, which was located about eight miles west of town.*[2]]
I slept there for two hours, borrowed a horse, and at 3 a.m. was
again en route to Washington. Soon the sun rose gloriously above
the summit of the Dragoon range and disclosed a marvelous array
of mountain landscapes. The happenings of the night before
loomed as a weird vision that seemed only to emphasize the
splendors of the morning. It was nearly eight o'clock in the
morning when I reached Benson.

Soon after breakfast I met Jimmie Harrington and thanked him
for not stopping the stage at the command of the bandits. "I'm
tellin' you, Mayor," said Jimmie, "you don't owe me nothin.' I
just couldn't hold them damned broncos. Didn't you hear the
brakes screechin'? Well, when they pulls the guns on me and tells
me to stop, it don't pay me to drive on, not at $35 per month." No,
I guess not, Jimmie.[3]

Riding back to Washington on the train alone I had a lot to
think about. I had declined to run for re-election as mayor. [*John
Carr was elected mayor of Tombstone on January 3, 1882, out-
polling Lewis W. Blinn.*[4]] For several months, ever since
Geronimo and Nah-chee broke loose from San Carlos and went on
the warpath, informal efforts had been made to get me to resume
charge of the Apaches at the agency. The "Epitaph" was not
excessively remunerative. The postmaster job involved hard work
and small pay. My wife had died at Tombstone. The outlaws and
the sheriff were too friendly for the good of the community. My
infant son was in Washington with my parents. What to do? I was
thirty years old now, but the problems were big.

Arriving in Washington just before Christmas, I read in the
newspapers that Fred Emerson Brooks had been appointed
postmaster at Tombstone. I thought I was still postmaster. So I

called on the first assistant postmaster general, Frank Hatton.

"How come you can appoint a postmaster where there is no vacancy?"

"Well, isn't there a vacancy?" he asked.

"Look me over, General. Do I appear to you as a vacancy?"

"You? Why, you have been reappointed Indian agent at San Carlos, have you not?"

"Not that I know of, General. Besides, I am not at all certain I care to return to San Carlos—not as long as the military has anything to do with the Indians. But I do need the post office job at Tombstone."

"I'll fix that immediately. You will be reappointed at once."

I was and my reappointment was duly confirmed by the Senate. This settled, I returned to Tombstone, arriving February 1, 1882. [*Clum's reinstatement as Tombstone's postmaster was never finalized, as he would discover in a few months.*[5]]

◇ ◇ ◇ ◇ ◇

Much had happened during my six week's absence. Sheriff Behan had made no progress toward apprehending the outlaws who held up [*fired upon*] the stage in December. Virgil Earp had been dangerously wounded. A night or two after Christmas [*on December 28, 1881*], Virgil was walking over to Carl Bilicke's hotel, the Cosmopolitan. The night was pitch black. As he passed the corner of Fifth and Allen streets, five of Ike Clanton's rustlers who had sneaked into town fired at him with short-barrel shotguns loaded with buckshot. Virgil's back was pretty well torn to pieces and a part of his [*left*] elbow had been shot away. Ambushed in the dark. He never fully recovered. Johnny Behan and his sheriff's office were never able to identify Virgil's assailants, much less capture them.

[*Upon learning of Virgil Earp's disabling injuries, U.S. Marshal for Arizona Crawley Dake (whose office was in Prescott, the territorial capital) commissioned Wyatt Earp a deputy U.S. marshal by telegraph.*[6] *This was Wyatt's first formal law enforcement position since he resigned as deputy Pima County sheriff in November 1880. (Wyatt's stint as Virgil's "special" deputy is classified here as an informal assignment.)*

Sheriff Behan had not been totally passive in response to the attack on Virgil Earp. Warrants were served on Ike and Phineas Clanton on the suspicion that they were involved, and on February 2, 1882, the brothers were examined before Judge

*William H. Stilwell (no relation to Frank Stilwell). A number of witnesses testified that the Clantons had been in Charleston on the night of the shooting, and Ike and Phin were then released.*⁷]

Looking west on Allen Street at the intersection of Allen and Fifth streets. Virgil Earp was ambushed as he crossed Fifth (right foreground), walking west, on the night of December 28, 1881. Photo taken about 1881. Arizona Historical society, Tucson, #60672.

Morgan Earp and Bob Hatch were playing pool one night [*in Campbell & Hatch's Billiard Parlor*] in March '82 [*March 18*]. Morgan liked to play pool and indulged frequently. Frank Stilwell, a Clanton satellite, knew of Morgan's habits and arranged with Indian Charlie and Pete Spence to help do the job. The feud was still on. As Morgan leaned over the pool table intent upon a difficult side-pocket shot, a different sort of shot rang out: a bullet crashed through the glass window at the rear of the billiard hall, then another. Morgan crumpled to the floor, his spine shattered. His three brothers Virgil, Wyatt, and Warren came running. "Who did it, Morg?" asked Wyatt, crouched on the floor beside his brother. Morgan whispered something to Wyatt and died. No one else heard the name. Wyatt pressed his hand on Morgan's forehead. "Good-bye, Morg," he said grimly. "I'll get him for you." [*A coroner's jury heard evidence regarding Morgan's murder and ruled that the likely culprits were Frank Stilwell, Pete Spence, a man known as "Indian Charlie," and possibly others.*⁸]

Next day the funeral party drove to Benson to take Morgan's

body to Colton, California, where the parents of the Earp boys lived. [*The Earps and their friends boarded the train at Contention City, which was located about ten miles west of Tombstone. A branch line running south from Benson had opened for service in February 1882.*[9]] Virgil and Jimmy Earp (and their wives), Wyatt, Doc Holliday; that was the party. Before leaving Tombstone, Wyatt made some quiet inquiries. He learned that Frank Stilwell left on horseback immediately after Morgan had been shot. Northwest, in the direction of Tucson, someone had told him.

When the funeral train arrived at Tucson, Wyatt and Doc Holliday stepped out to get some fresh air or something. Both carried guns. As the train started, a shot rang out. Wyatt and Doc Holliday came trotting down the platform and swung aboard. Next morning [*March 21, 1882*], Frank Stilwell was found alongside a box car in the railroad yards, dead.

[*Tucson saloon keeper and diarist George Hand viewed Stilwell's body on the morning of March 21 and wrote this in his journal: "Frank Stillwell [sic] was shot all over, the worst shot-up man that I ever saw. He was found a few hundred yards from the hotel on the railroad tracks. It is supposed to be the work of Doc Holliday and the Earps, but they were not found. Holliday and the Earps knew that Stillwell shot Morg Earp and they were bound to get him."[10] The* Epitaph *reported that Stilwell was in Tucson to testify before a grand jury regarding the September 1881 hold-up of the Bisbee stage.*[11]]

Morgan was buried. Virgil, crippled, decided to remain indefinitely at Colton. [*Virgil Earp lost the use of his left arm as a result of the December 28, 1881, shooting.*] Wyatt and Doc Holliday returned to Tombstone. But conditions in the old town were changing. Sheriff Behan received a warrant from Tucson demanding he arrest Wyatt and Doc for the murder of Stilwell. Behan tried to serve the warrant, but Wyatt declined to be arrested. "Johnny," said Wyatt, "I can't lick you and your outlaw friends and the politicians all combined. You have lied about me and done your damndest to get me killed for two years. I'm sick of your whole outfit. Besides, Frank Stilwell had two accomplices in Morg's murder. I want to catch up with them before they get too far away. I'm leaving Tombstone tomorrow, Johnny, for keeps. In the meantime neither you nor any of your gang would better lay a hand on me." They didn't.

Wyatt Earp, Doc Holliday, and three or four of their close friends rode down Allen Street slowly and on into the desert.

Passersby watched them in silence. They knew the story. Most of them still believed in Wyatt, but it was better so. As for Wyatt, he was not thinking of Tombstone. Indian Charlie and Pete Spence were somewhere in the mountains. Somewhere. [*Besides Doc Holliday, Wyatt's entourage included Warren Earp, Sherman McMasters, Texas Jack Vermillion, and Turkey Creek Jack Johnson.*[12]]

Within two hours Johnny Behan organized a posse composed mostly of known outlaws and rustlers. Curly Bill was in charge. [*Behan's posse included Phin Clanton, John Ringo, and others not kindly disposed toward the Earps, but Curly Bill was not identified as part of the group.*[13]] Pete Spence had a little ranch in the foothills of the Dragoons. Wyatt and his party passed that way. Indian Charlie was chopping wood. In the morning other wood-choppers found him with four bullet holes clear through him. [*A fellow named Florentino Cruz was killed at Pete Spence's camp on March 22.*[14] *Were Cruz and Indian Charlie one and the same man? Apparently Wyatt thought so. Spence himself escaped Wyatt's wrath.*[15]] Curly Bill's posse caught up with Wyatt's party and opened fire. The battle lasted five minutes. Quick shooting. One of Wyatt's bullets got Curly square in the forehead. So much for Curly Bill. The posse retreated.

[*The skirmish described above took place a few miles from Tombstone on March 24, 1882. Many people at the time questioned the claim that Curly Bill had been killed because his body was not brought to town and identified. There were reports that he was not even involved in the clash, and some people stated that he had left the territory weeks before the incident took place. But one thing is for sure—Curly Bill was not seen alive in Arizona again. Tombstone researchers are still on the lookout for definitive information about what happened to Curly Bill Brocius.*[16]]

Wyatt and his friends trekked northward into the dusk. We shall meet him again—in Alaska. [*The Earp party left the territory and sought refuge in Colorado, arriving there in April 1882. Arizona officials tried to bring Wyatt and Doc back to face murder charges but were unsuccessful.*[17]]

Early in 1882 the water level had been reached in the most important mines of the Tombstone district and the prosperity of the camp began sharply to decline. Sam Purdy and his associates submitted a proposition for the purchase of the "Epitaph." I decided to sell and devote my entire time to the post office. The sale was completed about the middle of May, and I at once settled down to the orderly life made possible by the fact that I was then responsible for only one job. [*Sam Purdy assumed the editorship of the* Tombstone Epitaph *on May 1, 1882, two years to the day after the first issue of the paper appeared. The new owners changed the* Epitaph *from a Republican organ to a Democratic one.*[18]]

The second big Tombstone fire started at three o'clock on the afternoon of May 25th in the vicinity of Fifth and Allen streets and destroyed a considerable portion of the business section bounded by Allen and Toughnut and Fourth and Fifth. Among the buildings destroyed were the Grand Hotel, the Cosmopolitan Hotel, Brown's Hotel, the "Nugget" newspaper office, and the Western Union Telegraph office. During the early part of the fire I was assisting with our man-power fire engine and otherwise. Finally, as the fire crept down toward Fourth Street, I returned to the post office. Although I really did not think that the building was in danger, I decided to remove everything from the office.

On account of the scarcity of water, several buildings had been dynamited in an effort to check the flames. The safe, all of the mail, and all portable fixtures had been removed, with the exception of one general delivery case. Dave Neagle, a deputy sheriff, came into the office through a rear door and told me he had placed a box of dynamite beneath the rear of the building and had lighted the fuse. Dave advised us to "get out." We did, and had only proceeded half a block when the dynamite exploded and the adobe walls of the post office were precipitated into the air. The post office was covered with a tin roof, which in its ascent and descent gave the effect of stage thunder. [*Dave Neagle had been a deputy sheriff, but on January 3, 1882, he was elected Tombstone's chief of police, defeating James Flynn and Leslie Blackburn.*[19]]

Immediately I obtained permission to occupy the Turn Verein Hall and transferred all the mail and the post office to that building. [*Turn Verein Hall was headquarters for German-American social activities. The name literally means "athletic club."*] When the mail arrived next morning, I arranged a semi-circle of benches in the front part of the hall. On these benches we placed a score of empty cigar boxes, which we labeled with the names of the principal patrons of the post office. This arrangement facilitated the distribution of the morning mail. When this mail

Two views of Tombstone after the May 25, 1882, fire. Upper image: looking southeast on Fremont Street. Lower image: looking northwest—Schieffelin Hall, undamaged, is at the upper right, the O.K. Corral signpost can be seen (faintly) at the far left. C. S. Fly photos, Arizona Historical Society, #42002 and #49697.

had been distributed, I glanced at a copy of the Tucson "Star" and was surprised to find in it a press dispatch from Washington stating that the controversy over the Tombstone post office had been settled finally by the commissioning of Fred Brooks as postmaster. I had graduated from a busy man with two official jobs and one private job to a very private citizen with no job at all.

[*It seems logical that there was more to the story of Clum's removal as Tombstone postmaster than he tells us here. By now he had plenty of political enemies who would have rejoiced at his joblessness. Nonetheless, in a previous chapter Clum described Fred Brooks as a fine fellow and clearly did not blame him for his predicament.*]

6

BOOMS AND DEPRESSIONS

It is fascinating to see an idea develop successfully. Booms and boom towns always have intrigued me. Participating in this sort of progress is romance . . . . A desert mountainside, barren save for cactus and mesquite and a few stray boulders eroded by the centuries. Silence. Great carrion birds soaring gracefully against the blue, their sharp eyes searching for victims in the scant desert growth. All else is motionless.

A lone prospector, bewhiskered and weary, is climbing the hill, his burro trailing leisurely. The two seem tiny in the tremendous landscape. The man stops occasionally, chips off bits of out-croppings with his small pick. He has been doing this for years . . . not on this mountainside but on hundreds of other mountain-sides in Arizona and New Mexico. Always weary, always hopeful, always unsuccessful.

But this time he has found it. The man and his burro disappear. They have taken fifty pounds of ore to the assayer to determine whether or not the long quest for fortune has ended. A week passes, two weeks. The man returns with a dozen burros loaded with provisions and mining equipment. A white tent looms on the mountainside. Two tents. A hundred tents. News of the discovery has traveled far. Other men have come, bewhiskered, hopeful, trailed by their burros. Wagons come loaded with lumber from distant forests. The boom has started. Dust clouds fill the valley from the plodding feet of merchants and artisans, pilgrims to the new Mecca. Streets are laid out. Homes and business blocks are built of lumber and of adobe. Smiles are on men's faces. Their hearts are light, made so by that greatest of magicians: prosperity.

This was the romance of Tombstone. Within six months ten thousand men had placed a city upon that desert mountainside. Silence of the unpeopled hills had been routed by the hum of industry. Curling smoke betrayed peaceful, happy firesides. Life was normal and we looked toward the future with optimism. The mountain was full of ore . . . we thought. So were all the surrounding mountains . . . we thought. And we re-invested our current profits because of what we thought. Tombstone in '80 and '81 was in full vigor, proud and hopeful. We who lived there in those days liked the town and its people.

Then came water, greatest single blessing of mankind but the

Looking northwest over Tombstone at the height of the boomtown's prosperity. Photo taken in 1881. Arizona Historical Society, Tucson, #42005.

curse of Tombstone. The mountain might be full of ore, but water held the miners back. Thou shalt not pass. Payrolls decreased. Unemployment increased. One by one, merchants closed their stores, nailed boards across the window fronts. Expert engineers were brought from afar to plan battle against the adamant enemy of the community. Fantastic ideas were promulgated. Build great syphons, bring the water out of the mines and spread it over the desert hillside and the desert valley. Then miners could get more ore, and in place of cactus and mesquite there would be orchards and gardens, roses and honeysuckle on the hillside and in the valley. Water the curse would become water the blessing. But that scheme went haywire. New types of pumps were suggested. Other cure-alls were suggested. None of them worked. Tombstone faded rapidly.

Then came the fire, ally of the water, to add its pressure to the burden of our people. My parents, sisters, and brothers lived in Washington, far removed from the tribulations of the frontier. I stood ankle deep in the ashes and dust of Tombstone, reflecting upon the fact that I was jobless and that the town was slipping fast. I was still able to smile, but my heart was heavy. I loved the West, the open spaces, the desert mountains, the illusions and disillusions. Friends had written me from Washington that a job awaited me there in the Post Office Department. That meant a swivel chair in an office, street cars, the din of small things in a big city. I had spent eleven years in Arizona and New Mexico, the plastic years of early manhood. I had become a frontiersman to the marrow. But I had to have a job and there were no jobs in Tombstone. Then one evening [*probably in June 1882[1]*] I took the stage over to Benson [*more likely to Contention City*], boarded the train to Washington, the home folks, and the swivel chair.

[*Clum's assertion that the Tombstone mines were in decline as early as 1882 is not correct. His personal fortunes may have been sagging, but 1882 was the year of peak silver production in the area. Although water had been noticed in the deepest shafts as early as 1881, it did not become troublesome until about 1883. In that year huge Cornish pumps were installed in the Contention and Grand Central mines, two of the largest producers, and the yield of silver held up fairly well for a while. But by 1884 it was clear that Tombstone's glory days were over. Labor disputes added to the mine owners' problems, and the price of silver began to decline. In May 1886 a fire destroyed the Grand Central's pump works and hoisting apparatus and the mine closed. The Contention Mine shut down in August 1886 owing to the low price of silver. The Tombstone mining boom had come to an end.[2]*]

◇ ◇ ◇ ◇ ◇

I married Miss Belle Atwood in Washington in February '83, and the night before Christmas '83 a daughter [*Caro*] was born. I attended evening lectures at the National Medical College. I joined the Lawrence Barrett dramatic club and stalked the amateur stage along with Charlie Hanford and Wilton Lackaye. I tried to adapt myself to the ways of a big city. But I kept in touch with the affairs of the West. Some new scheme had been projected to save the mining industry of Tombstone, a scheme that seemed practical. Tombstone renewed its hope and some of its vigor. I wanted to go back and help in the rejuvenation. I mentioned this to Frank Hatton, who still was postmaster general. A few days later I was again appointed postmaster at Tombstone.

[*President Arthur promoted Frank Hatton from assistant postmaster general to postmaster general in October 1884. He served until Grover Cleveland's inauguration as president in March 1885.[3] Clum's appointment as Tombstone postmaster was effective January 20, 1885. He succeeded Fred Brooks, the man who had replaced him in 1882.[4]*]

◇ ◇ ◇ ◇ ◇

In February '85 I was back on the old job where, five years before, a city had grown overnight on the side of a desert mountain. Familiar streets, a few familiar faces. Prosperity seemed just around the corner. But the new scheme for removing water from the mines was no better than its predecessors. Tombstone suffered a relapse. You know how it is when a person who has been very ill makes a rally, holds his own for a week or two, then begins to slip again. Well, the same psychology prevailed in Tombstone. The most persistent optimists skulked in shadows of gloom. The final curtain was about to be rung down.

[*Belle and Caro accompanied John to Tombstone; Woodworth stayed in Washington with his grandparents. On February 7, 1886, a Sunday, Caro was baptized. It isn't clear exactly where the ceremony took place, but St. Paul's Episcopal Church is the most likely location. George Parsons, a devout church-goer, commented on the event in his diary: "Before the service several children were baptized and I was Godfather to Mrs. Clum's little one, Caroline Kingsley [Kingsland] Clum. She is two years old and a bright little thing. 'What's that Papa?' she kept repeating, pointing to the bowl."5*]

The Clums at their home in Tombstone. Left to right: John, Belle, and Caro. John P. Clum Collection, Special Collections Department, University of Arizona Library.

More storefronts were boarded up, more homes deserted. My post-office salary was reduced painfully when the office was made third class. So I resigned and became city auditor and ex-officio police judge. [*Clum resigned as postmaster effective October 5, 1885, and was appointed city auditor/recorder on October 7, 1885.*[6]] Being police judge saved me from the slough of despond. Interesting cases involving cross sections of what was left of the town of Tombstone were heard almost every day. While the population had dwindled from 10,000 to 4,000 [*in reality from about 5,000 to 2,000 people*], we still had our share of saloons, gambling halls, and gamblers. But the gambling had to be honest, if you know what I mean. No sleight of hand stuff, no trickery, no cheating. While I knew how the various games of chance were played, I had never gambled myself. That early Holland-Dutch-Reform training, perhaps. That, and the fact that always I was compelled to conserve my finances.

Two faro dealers had been arrested and hauled before me charged with operating a crooked faro game. In faro, you know, the cards are dealt from a little box just large enough to hold the cards. The box is supposed to permit the dealer to draw off only one card at a time. If the dealer should draw off two cards at once, the house couldn't lose. These two gamblers were charged with using a trick box, but they went on the witness stand and swore the box was honest and that their faro game was straight. We adjourned court at noon for luncheon, and inasmuch as the alleged trick box had been submitted as evidence, I took it with me and did some experimenting. And I discovered the trick. When court reconvened, I told the gamblers I thought the box was crooked and proceeded to deal out cards, as in a faro game. "If you think it's crooked, Judge, let's see you deal two cards at once," challenged one of them. They knew I never gambled and thought they had me licked. But I deftly unlocked the trick box and dealt out two cards. And, of course, I held the gamblers for the grand jury.

While such cases as this helped me keep my mind off the depression then rampant in Tombstone, it did not help the rest of the surviving citizens. They were very much in the dumps. So we devised all sorts of social activities. Whistling in the graveyard, as it were. Some of the amateur plays that we presented in Schieffelin Hall went over big, not only providing entertainment for audiences and actors, but also helping local charities through box-office receipts. Our most pretentious performance was "Esmeralda" [*staged February 18, 1886*[7]]. I took the part of "Esterbrook," and, in the course of three acts, wooed and won

Now little played, faro was a popular game of chance in the late 1800s. This photo of a faro layout was taken in a Morenci, Arizona, saloon circa 1890. Arizona Historical Society, Tucson, #2819.

"Nora Desmond" impersonated by Mrs. [Bessie] McNeil.[8] Mrs. McNeil and I each had an infant-in-arms at our respective homes, but, of course, we had to forget this while we were on the stage. The third act called for the emotional climax when Esterbrook placed the ring upon Nora's finger and imprinted a lover's kiss upon her lips. Naturally, we had to rehearse the play many times and Mr. [Donald A.] McNeil and Mrs. Clum always were present at rehearsals. In an effort to get even with us, our respective mates threatened to bring our respective infants to the public performance. More than that, they proposed to walk down the center aisle, side by side, at the emotional moment of the third act, bearing the babes in their arms. Good comedy, yes, but tough on the amateur actors who were supposed to be immersed in romance. When the big night arrived, and the third act arrived, I slipped the ring on Mrs. McNeil's finger, keeping one eye on the center aisle. But nothing happened and I completed the job in accepted fashion. Happily, our mates had lost their courage.

◇ ◇ ◇ ◇ ◇

In putting ore through a mill, the precious metals are held in vats or trays, while the refuse rock goes out the flume and forms great piles outside the mill. This refuse is called "tailings." Mill methods then in vogue left considerable silver in the tailings. Ed Wilson came to me one day and explained a patent he had acquired for extracting precious metals from tailings. So Ed, Dan O'Connor, and I formed a partnership and went into the mining business.

Although I had been in Tombstone off and on for six years, this was my first mining venture. We built a "reduction" plant, well named, as I soon discovered. Proper proportions of Ed's patented solution and tailings were placed in a large cask which was revolved rapidly for ten minutes. The power was supplied by a horse driven by Dan. After the violent shake-up, the mixture was drained carefully into a settling tank. After it settled we were supposed to scoop up lots of silver at the retort. For two months we worked, Dan, Ed, I, and the horse. But the solution did not work. As a reduction plant, ours was a complete success in that our joint and several bank accounts had been reduced to the vanishing point. We even saw red—$1,500 worth. Inasmuch as the solution did not dissolve the tailings, we dissolved the partnership and sold the horse. And I stayed away from mining ventures until they hooked me in Nome [*Alaska*] in 1900.

Things were getting desperate again. Tombstone was rapidly assuming all of the habiliments of a ghost town—entire blocks in the business section with all storefronts boarded up. Picket fences around deserted houses on the edge of town were torn up and used for firewood. Then, slowly, some of the frame houses followed the fate of the fences. Tombstone was on its last legs. Dan O'Connor showed me a Los Angeles newspaper giving glowing accounts of the boom that was under way in southern California. Lots of action there, the paper said, lots of jobs, lots of opportunities. So Dan and I went to Benson and boarded the train for San Bernardino. Good town in those days, up and coming, and it still is. [*Clum abdicated his municipal posts on November 13, 1886, and he and his family said good-bye to Tombstone soon thereafter.9*]

Soon the real estate and insurance firm of Clum & O'Connor announced itself. A boom was on, sure enough. We prospered and moved into spacious quarters on the ground floor of the Stewart Hotel block. Believing in the future of the community, I immediately re-invested all my profits, save only living expenses, and bought more land to make more profits to buy more land. That is a fine formula, as long as the boom lasts.

The San Bernardino office of the firm of Clum & O'Connor. John P. Clum Collection, Special Collections Department, University of Arizona Library.

For one of our clients we sold a ranch for $12,000 on the prevailing terms of $4,000 cash, $4,000 in six months, and $4,000 in a year. We drew up a contract for a deed to be delivered upon completion of the deferred payments.

"But what security have I for the payment of the other $8,000?" queried our client.

"You will not deed over the ranch until all payments have been made," we advised him.

"Yes, I know," he replied, "but what security have I for the payment of the $8,000?"

"You still own the ranch until the remaining $8,000 is paid," we again told him.

"Yes, I know," he persisted, "but the ranch is not worth $8,000."

We had no good answer for that, but we should have had, for

that was the danger signal and we never saw it at all. Looking backward, I recall that prices had become so inflated that every real estate sale was made at from one-third to one-half above actual value. My conscience does not bother me for selling to our clients at these high prices, because the apparently prosperous firm of Clum & O'Connor bought all the acreage it could get hold of on the same exorbitant basis. Booms are funny things. Your belief in the brilliant future of the booming community becomes so intense that you develop boom-blindness. You see nothing but permanent prosperity. Everybody in town is a booster, a boomer, an optimist. Any man who expresses a belief that the boom may burst some day is branded a knocker and chased out of town. It was the same psychology that built up stock prices in 1929 and you know what happened then.

EDITOR'S EPILOGUE

John Clum's life after leaving Arizona was rarely routine, but being an Apache agent during Geronimo's heyday and mayor of Tombstone at the time of the "Gunfight at the O.K. Corral" were hard acts to follow. As he related in the previous chapter, the southern California land boom didn't last. As in Tombstone, people were millionaires one day and paupers the next. After land prices crashed in the fall of 1888 and his real estate firm went bust, Clum had to scramble to make ends meet. Always light on his feet and never at a loss for ideas, he worked out a deal with the San Bernardino County Board of Trade to act as a publicist for the fledgling citrus industry. It was hoped that oranges would revitalize the depressed local economy and restore land values. Clum toured southern California soliciting contributions for his citrus advertising campaign. To acquaint East Coast consumers (and, hopefully, investors) with West Coast products, in February 1890 Clum mounted a lavish produce exhibit in New York City. The display included two-dozen large, potted orange trees in fruit. The presentation was a hit but citrus promotion did not blossom into a career. Clum was hired as an assistant editor for the San Francisco *Examiner* in the spring of 1890, but he did not find working for the newspaper to be very satisfactory. In June 1890 he secured a job as a civilian clerk in the Washington offices of the War Department, and the Clums moved to the East.

In January 1891 Clum accepted an appointment as an inspector (a kind of detective) for the U.S. Postal Service. As a postal cop, Clum investigated crooks who robbed the mails or used them to carry out illegal schemes. During the next four years he chased thieves and exposed con artists in Kentucky, West Virginia, Texas, and South Carolina. In 1894 he was promoted to a desk job in Washington. He wrote: "Having spent 23 years in the wide open spaces peopled by Apaches and outlaws and mail robbers, this office job seemed quite tame. Time hung heavy, so I went into the illustrated lecture business on the side. My forte was our own United States. My slogan was 'See America First.' I had lots of fun, made a little extra cash, and kept busy." Clum was active with Washington's amateur theater groups as well.

In 1896 gold was discovered in the Klondike region of Yukon Territory and soon the rush to the Northwest was on. The center of activity was in western Yukon near the Canada-Alaska border, but there were strikes across the line in Alaska as well. Much like

John P. Clum Collection, Special Collections Department, University of Arizona Library.

Cochise County twenty years earlier, settlements were springing up in the wilderness and they required postal services. By the winter of '97-98 it had become clear that someone from Washington needed to go to Alaska and supervise the expansion of post office activities there. Although now in his late forties the spirit of adventure was still alive and well in John Clum, and he eagerly volunteered to undertake the mission. He described his feelings this way: "The old frontier fever began creeping over me. Sitting at a desk all day, giving illustrated lectures occasionally in the evenings, did not measure up to my idea of a job. Alaska . . . trails . . . mountains . . . running waters . . . campfires . . . open spaces. That's the life!" Clum was appointed special postal inspector for Alaska and he hastily began making preparations to visit the remote territory. He kept a diary during his 1898 trip to Alaska and it is now in the archives of University of Arizona Library.

On his way west John Clum picked up his son, Woodworth, who was a student at Case Western Reserve University in Cleveland. The two reached Seattle on March 17, 1898. Before long they were in Skagway, Alaska, gateway to the upper Yukon River, the Klondike, and untold riches. For several weeks John

Clum traveled about southern Alaska inspecting postal operations in Skagway, Dyea, Fort Wrangell, Juneau, Haines, and other coastal towns. But soon it would be time to head for the interior and the new gold fields.

In order to reach eastern Alaska the men needed to cross a portion of Yukon Territory. But a forbidding mountain range towered over the Alaska panhandle and it could only be traversed on foot. In early April John Clum decided to reconnoiter the famous Dyea Trail through Chilkoot Pass, the route being taken by thousands of eager treasure seekers. The Clums arrived at Dyea, a few miles from Skagway, then hiked to Sheep Camp at the foot of the trail that led up into the pass. On April 5 they started up the trail but were forced back by a nasty snowstorm. The next day they climbed to the summit of the pass. The trail was clogged with men, toiling upward, the lure of gold irresistible. The steep slopes were heavy with snow, and on the way back to Sheep Camp the Clums came upon a throng of men feverishly digging in the white mass. An avalanche had swept a number of luckless prospectors away to their deaths. John and Woodworth pitched in and helped rescue the survivors and exhume the dead. Clum noted in his diary that fifty-two bodies were recovered from the avalanche debris.

Packers trudge toward the summit of Chilkoot Pass. Photo taken in 1898. John P. Clum Collection, Special Collections Department, University of Arizona Library.

On May 19, with heavy packs on their backs, John and Woodworth struggled up and over Chilkoot Pass. At the summit another snowstorm greeted them. After the mountain pass was negotiated, canoes took the Clums down to the Yukon River, and there they boarded a boat that transported them the five hundred miles to Dawson. Situated at the junction of the Yukon and Klondike rivers, Dawson was a boom town much like Tombstone had been in the '80s. They arrived at the town on June 21. John Clum described the scene in his diary: "The thousands of boats on the riverfront and streets thronged with humanity and the scores of tents, cabins, and caches which specked the hillsides presented a pleasing and unique picture. Dawson is the Coney Island of the Northwest." Clum ran into an old friend in Dawson, Nellie Cashman. She too had joined the gold rush and was running a boarding house and helping the needy in the raw mining town.

Ellen "Nellie" Cashman (1845-1925) in Dawson, Yukon Territory. Photo taken by John Clum in 1898. Arizona Historical Society, Tucson, #1134.

After consulting with Canadian officials about coordinating mail delivery throughout the Yukon-Alaska gold region, John and

Woodworth headed west, left Canada, and entered Alaska for the second time on their trip. The following weeks were hectic ones as Clum traveled about the territory establishing new post offices and appointing postmasters to run them. In late August the Clums returned to the States.

The Nome post office in 1900. The bald chap in the center of the room is John Clum. John P. Clum Collection, Special Collections Department, University of Arizona Library.

John Clum was sent to Alaska again in 1900. Gold strikes kept people coming, and the Postal Service was hard pressed to meet its obligations. While making his rounds inspecting post offices, Clum ran into his old friend Wyatt Earp. The former lawman, in partnership with a man named Charles Hoxie, had opened the Dexter Saloon in Nome shortly after gold was discovered nearby. George Parsons, who also had migrated north, wrote this in his diary on August 30, 1900: "John Clum, Fowler & I had an old timer with Wyatt Earp tonight @ his place. A regular old Arizona time & Wyatt unlimbered for several hours. Seemed glad to talk to us who knew the past." Earp made good money in Nome selling whiskey to miners, more than most of his customers accumulated searching for gold. But he didn't stay long and by 1902 was plying his trade as a gambler and saloon keeper in

Wyatt Earp (left) and John Clum on the beach at Nome, Alaska.
Photo taken in 1900. John P. Clum Collection, Special Collections
Department, University of Arizona Library.

Nevada.

In the fall of 1900 Clum was transferred from Washington to the New York Division of the Postal Service. He spent the next six winters in New York City, the warm months in Alaska. New Yorkers were treated to many a lecture on Alaska and the gold rush put on by showman Clum. In 1902 Belle and Caro went with John to the Far North and spent a summer in the land of the midnight sun. The next year Clum succumbed to temptation and invested some of his hard-earned salary in an Alaska mining venture, but his speculation didn't pan out.

Early in 1906 President Theodore Roosevelt began shopping around for a replacement for Alaska governor John Brady, and Clum made it known that he wanted the job. Clum was liked and respected by Alaskans—they knew he had worked hard on their behalf—and Roosevelt seriously considered him for the appointment. But in March 1906 the president chose Wilford Hoggatt for the governorship.

Clum was named postmaster of Fairbanks in August 1906. He and Belle lived in the frigid central Alaska town for nearly three years. While there, Postmaster Clum gave lectures and performed in several amateur theatricals to the delight of local audiences. Caro Clum, now in her twenties, accompanied her parents to Alaska and on September 2, 1908, married merchant Peter A. Vachon in Fairbanks.

In 1908 John Clum again tried his hand at politics. This time he had his eye on the position of delegate to Congress from Alaska. Clum ran for delegate as an Independent but did poorly, finishing a disappointing last in a field of five candidates. Republican James Wickersham won the contest and went on to serve several terms as Alaska's congressional representative.

Like all such extravaganzas, the Klondike-Alaska gold rush eventually petered out. By 1909 the excitement was over and it was time for people with "Tombstone" in their blood to depart. In June Clum quit his job as Fairbanks' postmaster and he and Belle returned to the lower states. (Clum had tendered his resignation as postmaster in October 1908, but it was not accepted until the following June.) He worked as a postal inspector in Washington State and Colorado, and gave lectures on his Alaska adventures when time permitted. Clum resigned from the Postal Service in April 1911.

John Clum was now sixty years old but he was not ready to retire. The Southern Pacific Railroad was embarking on an aggressive advertising campaign aimed at tourists. Who better to present the company's message about "The Road of a Thousand Wonders" on the lecture circuit than John Clum? In the spring of 1911 Clum accepted the position of railroad publicist and began traveling throughout the country, speaking on behalf of the Southern Pacific and the grandeur of his beloved West.

In September 1912 Belle Clum, John's second wife, died. In October 1914 Clum married Florence Baker, a woman twenty years his junior. He met Florence in New York during one of his speaking engagements. In 1915 the Clums purchased a twenty-acre date plantation in the hot and dry Coachella Valley, about 125 miles east of Los Angeles. Clum was truly interested in horticulture, and when not lecturing he carefully tended his special "Deglet Noor" palms.

Clum was not totally satisfied with his job as spokesman for the Southern Pacific. From 1912 to 1917 he carried on extensive correspondence with the commissioner of Indian affairs in an attempt to rejoin the Indian Bureau. Clum had decided that he would like to be superintendent of an Indian school somewhere in the Southwest or possibly return to his former position as Indian agent. The Washington officials politely put him off, gently telling him that times had changed and it was a younger generation's turn to handle such assignments.

During World War I civilian travel over the railroads was curtailed and so were Clum's promotional tours. The S.P. kept him busy by giving him a job as a railroad security official. After the war Clum resumed lecturing, then retired from full-time work in 1920 at the age of sixty-nine. Upon retirement John and Florence settled down on their date farm. After a couple of years they traded the date grove for a small citrus and chicken ranch near San Dimas. In 1928, owing to John's advancing age, they swapped the San Dimas property for a house in nearby Los Angeles. Without the orange grove to oversee, Clum had time on his hands and he returned to writing. Soon lengthy articles detailing his youthful experiences in Arizona and New Mexico began appearing in historical journals.

Wyatt Earp and his third wife, Josephine, also lived in Los Angeles in the 1920s. During the final year of his life the old frontiersman kept in close touch with Clum, the editor who steadfastly supported him during his darkest hours in Arizona. Earp died at his home on January 13, 1929. Clum served as an honorary pall bearer at Wyatt's funeral.

In October 1929 Clum returned to Cochise County as an honored guest at Tombstone's first "Helldorado Days" celebration. The population of Tombstone had shrunk to about 850 souls, and the town fathers knew that the community desperately needed a lift. Hopefully Helldorado, celebrating Tombstone's fiftieth anniversary, would help. As part of the festivities, townspeople in costume reenacted the "Gunfight at the O.K. Corral." Despite his love of showmanship, Clum was not amused. He felt it was wrong to glorify such a grisly event. The former

Tombstone mayor did not realize that the legendary shootout had become the struggling town's greatest asset.

John Clum and an Apache friend at San Carlos in 1931. John P. Clum Collection. Special Collections Department, University of Arizona Library.

Accompanied by his son, Woodworth (who now lived in Los Angeles), and two friends, Dr. Clarence Toland and Harry Carr, John Clum visited the San Carlos Reservation in 1931. The Bureau of Reclamation had completed Coolidge Dam on the Gila River and the site of the old San Carlos Agency would soon be

covered by a lake. San Carlos was the setting for some of the elder
Clum's most daring and controversial exploits, and he wanted to
see the place one last time. Two men who had served in Clum's
Apache police force were still alive, Sneezer and Goodah-Goodah,
and the three old warriors spent long hours telling stories of past
achievements to a large crowd of listeners.

*Sneezer (left) and Goodah-Goodah served in John Clum's Apache
police force in the 1870s. John P. Clum Collection, Special
Collections Department, University of Arizona Library.*

On May 2, 1932, John Philip Clum died suddenly at his Los
Angeles home. He had outlived most of the people he wrote about
in his account of Tombstone's wild and wooly heyday. The Earp
brothers, Doc Holliday, Ike Clanton, Johnny Behan, Billy
Breakenridge, Ed and Al Schieffelin, Richard Gird, Nellie
Cashman, his old nemesis, Geronimo—all preceded him in death.
One of Clum's friends from the old days outlived him. George
Parsons had attended Mary Clum's funeral in Tombstone and fifty
years later was present at John Clum's in Los Angeles. Parsons
passed away the next year at the age of eighty-two.

John Clum, the boomer, the promoter, the eternal optimist, the tireless wanderer in search of the pot of gold at the end of the rainbow, never got rich in the West. Or did he? During his eight decades of life he acquired a wealth of fast friends and some of the best enemies imaginable. John Clum's life was rich with adventure, something more precious than silver or gold.

PART II

John Clum and the Apaches

Geronimo on the loose in northern Sonora. Detail from a photo taken by C. S. Fly in March 1886. Arizona Historical Society, Tucson, #78153.

7

THE CAPTURE OF GERONIMO

Editor's note: When John Clum decided to train and arm an Apache police force and give it the job of keeping order on the San Carlos Reservation, many people thought he was crazy. Although General George Crook had used Apache scouts to good effect in the early 1870s, his Apache soldiers were but a small part of a larger military command. As proposed, Clum's Apache police would far outnumber Whites at San Carlos, and if they proved disloyal the consequences could be disastrous. However, to the dismay of everyone except Clum, his native policemen distinguished themselves as reliable and capable law enforcers. The most notable achievements of Clum's Apache police were: the transfer of a number of Chiricahua Apaches from their reservation in the southeastern corner of Arizona to San Carlos in June 1876; the arrest in April 1877 of the Chiricahua leader Geronimo, who had resisted being uprooted and moved north to the Gila River.

The Chiricahua Reservation was established in 1872 as part of the terms of a peace treaty agreed upon by General Oliver O. Howard and Cochise. Frontiersman Tom Jeffords, a friend of Cochise, was hired as agent for the Chiricahuas. Eventually between six and seven hundred people came under Jeffords' supervision. Two distinct groups, the "Central Chiricahua" and "Southern Chiricahua" bands, were settled on the reserve. Cochise was undisputed chief of the Central Chiricahua band; Geronimo was a Southern Chiricahua warlord. Cochise died in 1874, and his eldest son, Taza, assumed his place of leadership.

Under Jeffords' regime the Chiricahuas made little progress toward becoming civilized, and his superiors wanted a change. In 1876 an episode of violence involving a few unruly Apaches led by a warrior named Pionsenay gave government officials the excuse they had been looking for to renege on the treaty made with Cochise. They abolished the reservation, fired Agent Jeffords, and ordered John Clum to take the Chiricahuas to San Carlos and add them to the more than 4,000 people already congregated there. Thus Geronimo and Clum were brought together by forces beyond either man's control.

In the following story, Clum describes his initial encounter with Geronimo and his capture of the renegade a year later. It

*was first published under the title "Geronimo" in the January
1928 issue of the* New Mexico Historical Review.

Apache Pass will ever be intimately associated with Apache
Indian history and especially with the life stories of Cochise and
Geronimo. There, for two or three decades, the former was a
dominant figure as chief of the [*Central*] Chiricahuas, and there, a
little later, the latter made his debut as a notorious renegade.

Many of our readers may not at once recall the exact location
of Apache Pass, but if a little more than half a century ago they
had been travelers along the old Southern Overland Stage Road
between El Paso and San Diego they would distinctly remember
this pass as the most dangerous section of that route because of
frequent and savage attacks by bands of marauding Apaches. The
pass is a picturesque depression or divide in southeastern Arizona,
separating the Chiricahua Mountains on the south from the Dos
Cabezas range on the north, affording reasonably easy grades for
the famous overland highway, which for so many years threaded a
sinuous course through its scenic defiles.

In those early days—about 1860 [*1862*]—a small detachment
of United States troops arrived in Apache Pass and established a
military post in the midst of the canyon recesses, which later
became known as Fort Bowie. In 1872, by special order of
General O. O. Howard, the Chiricahua Indian Agency was located
about a mile west of the fort. And there I found these two
important government outposts when I first visited that historic
section in June 1876.

In February 1874 President Grant commissioned me agent for
the Apaches at the San Carlos Agency, which is located on the
Gila River at its confluence with the Rio San Carlos and about 150
miles northwest from Apache Pass. Nearly all of the Indians then
at the San Carlos Agency were known as Aravaipa Apaches. In
that same year, and prior to my arrival in Arizona, Cochise died,
so that I never had the opportunity of meeting the noted chief—a
fact I deeply regretted. [*Cochise died in June 1874.*] On My
arrival at San Carlos in August 1874, I found about 800 Indians
assembled on that reservation. Soon after, several small bands
were brought in from the adjacent mountains, which increased the
number under my direction to about 1,000.

In March 1875 the Indians from the Rio Verde Reservation
situated near Prescott were removed to San Carlos and placed in

my charge. There were about 1,400 of these Indians, comprising nearly equal numbers of Tontos and Mohaves—with a few Yumas. [*The people Clum referred to as Mohaves and Yumas undoubtedly were Yavapais.¹*] In July 1875, under orders from the Interior Department, I removed 1,800 Coyotero Apaches from the Camp Apache Agency, locating about half of these adjacent to the main agency at San Carlos and the remainder at a sub-agency on the Gila about twenty miles east of San Carlos. Thus it will appear that within a year the number of Apaches under my charge and direction increased from 800 to approximately 4,200.

John Clum and an escort of Apache police. John P. Clum Collection, Special Collections Department, University of Arizona Library.

Cochise left two sons, Tah-zay [*Taza*] and Nah-chee [*Naiche*]. After his death a bitter rivalry developed between Tah-zay, the elder son, and Skin-yea [*Skinya*], who had served as a war-chief under Cochise, as to who should succeed to the leadership of the tribe [*the Central Chiricahuas*]. The government officials recognized Tah-zay, but this action, instead of settling the controversy, only widened the breach between these stalwart aspirants and established an enmity which was destined to culminate in mortal combat.

Peace was maintained for about two years after the death of Cochise, but on April 6, 1876, a raiding party led by Pi-on-se-nay, a brother of Skin-yea, attacked the Overland Stage Station at Sulphur Springs, twenty-six miles west of Fort Bowie, killed two men named [*Nick*] Rogers and [*O. O.*] Spence, and committed other depredations in the San Pedro valley. Lieut. [*Austin*] Henely, with a troop of cavalry from Fort Bowie, followed the trail of these renegades for some days and finally overtook them near the Mexican border, but did not succeed in inflicting any punishment upon them.

Nearly a month after this outbreak I received the following telegraphic orders from the Commissioner of Indian Affairs:

> Washington, D.C.
> May 3, 1876
>
> Agent Clum,
> San Carlos, Arizona.
>
> Appropriation made by Congress. Will arrange for additional supplies. Proceed to Chiricahua; take charge of Indians and agency property there, suspending Agent Jeffords, for which this dispatch shall be your full authority. If practicable, remove Chiricahua Indians to San Carlos. For that purpose use not exceeding three thousand dollars. Governor Safford has been advised.
>
> J. Q. Smith,
> Commissioner

Before entering actively upon the execution of these orders I insisted that a sufficient military force should be ordered into the field to afford ample protection to settlers in any emergency. General August V. Kautz, commanding the Department of Arizona, hesitated, but upon receipt of orders from the War Department he sent the entire Sixth Cavalry into southern Arizona.

I chanced to be in Tucson when the above telegram from Washington was received there. Having made my request to

General Kautz for military support in the field, I proceeded at once over the trail (125 miles) to San Carlos for the purpose of organizing a special police force to accompany me to Apache Pass. About a week later I was back in Tucson with an escort of fifty-four Aravaipa and Coyotero braves, who constituted my personal bodyguard and free-lance army. [*Interpreter Merejildo Grijalva, who was fluent in the Apache language, accompanied Clum and his cadre of police on this important mission. Grijalva's assistance would be essential during negotiations with the Chiricahuas.*[2]]

Brevet Major General August V. Kautz (1828-1895) commanded the Department of Arizona from March 1875 to March 1878. He found Apache Agent John Clum a tough pill to swallow. Arizona Historical Society, Tucson, #19603.

While waiting for the cavalry to arrive in the field, the citizens of Tucson had an excellent opportunity to observe the character and conduct of my Apache police at close quarters. Since the organization of this police force at San Carlos in August 1874, its members had rendered most valuable service on the reservation, and reports of their efficiency and dependability had spread throughout the territory. But the average citizen of Arizona had visualized this force only at long range. Hence, when this company of fifty-four stalwart Apache police—fully armed and equipped for action—marched into the ancient and honorable pueblo of Tucson, they presented a unique and impressive spectacle, and the onlookers were fully persuaded that the reports of their efficiency and prowess had not been exaggerated.

During this period of "watchful waiting" for the Sixth Cavalry to arrive in the field, a committee of Tucson's leading citizens came to me with a request for an Apache war dance—they were eager to witness a genuine spectacle of this character. Would the visiting police oblige them? I consulted the police and found them not only willing but enthusiastic. Accordingly, the date for the "outbreak" was set. On the day appointed [*May 26*] a load of wood was hauled in to the center of the old Military Plaza [*the site of Camp Lowell until 1873*], and as soon as it was dark the camp-fire was kindled. Forthwith, the spectators began filing into the plaza by scores and hundreds until we had an expectant audience estimated at fully 3,000. The stage was set—on with the dance!

And now appeared the grotesque actors—thirty-five robust Apache braves stripped to the waist, their bodies and faces hideous with streaks and smears of war-paint, some wearing fantastic headgear, and each bearing either a lance and shield or a bow and arrow or a rifle, according to the act assigned. Accompanying these were the chanters and musicians with their tom-toms. The instruments all being in "tune," the first act was precipitated without hesitation or delay. This was a scene in which a lithe dancer performed gracefully with lance and shield. Gradually the number of active participants increased until the campfire was circled by a score or more of wildly gesticulating figures of ferocious aspect, and the night air was vibrant with a discordant chorus of blood-curdling war-whoops.

The committee had expressed their eager desire for a genuine spectacle, and when I observed the audience gradually retreating from the circle of lunging and howling performers I suspected that the play was becoming a bit too realistic to suit the fancy of the average "paleface." Presently Chief Justice [*Charles*] French edged his way to my side and, with an expression of unfeigned alarm and the tone of a veteran pleader, he said: "Clum, hadn't you better stop this before the Indians get beyond your control?" I replied (with apologies to John Paul Jones), "Why, Judge, we have just begun to dance."

And now the climax was approaching—for which our infatuated audience was wholly unprepared. None knew that I had supplied a half-dozen blank cartridges for each rifle in the custody of this apparently frantic bunch of athletic savages. Suddenly the sharp crack of a rifle echoed keen and clear above the din of the frenzied dance. This was the signal for a chorus of super-yells, and then BANG! BANG! BANG! BANG! came the nerve-racking explosions from some twenty additional rifles fired in volleys or in rapid succession. Meanwhile, the vocal exercises and athletic contortions of our unrestrained entertainers approached the peak of noise and confusion. To the average spectator it looked as if these unleashed representatives of the famed San Carlos Apache police were running amuck.

Fortunately, the old Military Plaza afforded ample exits for our now near terror-stricken audience. That was no place for a minister's son. No benediction or recessional was necessary, and although the retreat was orderly, we very soon realized that our enthusiastic audience had quite spontaneously and almost unanimously deserted the "auditorium" without according to our perfect performance the usual complimentary prolonged applause.

[*Tucson saloon keeper George Hand attended the show. He wrote the following in his diary on May 26, 1876: "Very warm—cloudy and sultry. Tom Roddick and Stroud came in town and both got drunk. I kept tolerably sober. Big things tonight—an Apache war dance. I went in company with Mr. O'Reilly to see the dance at 8 o'clock in the evening. It smelt so strong and wild that we only stayed a few moments."*[3]]

The citizens of Tucson were so well pleased with the general deportment of the police during their entire visit there that a purse was raised by popular subscription and the company presented with uniforms—white pants, red shirts, and an obsolete style of army hat. Not an expensive outfit, but highly valued as expressing friendliness and good will.

As soon as General Kautz arrived in Tucson he sent his aide, Colonel [*Major James P.*] Martin, to me with a request that I indicate how I thought the troops should be assigned in the field. When I demurred, Colonel Martin insisted that the commanding general was very desirous that I should express my judgement in the matter. This I finally did. [*Kautz and Clum were not on good terms. The general, of German birth, was offended by the young Indian agent's outspoken manner and apparent lack of proper respect for his seniority and rank.*]

The capture of the murderers of Rogers and Spence and the contemplated removal of the Chiricahua Indians to San Carlos were regarded as enterprises of more or less formidable proportions, and the campaign was not undertaken without serious misgivings. The very name of the Chiricahua Apaches had been a terror to the citizens of Arizona, New Mexico, and Sonora for many, many years. Scores of graves in this Southwestern region

John Clum (foreground) and a company of Apache police in Tucson, May 1876. The man at the far left is Merejildo Grijalva. Arizona Historical Society, Tucson, #924.

marked the final resting place of their victims. It was variously estimated that this tribe could muster from three hundred to five hundred able warriors—all well armed, brave and experienced. For more than a decade under Cochise they had successfully defied the troops—both American and Mexican—and had been victorious in almost every engagement with these troops. Skinyea, the old war-chief under Cochise, was still living and still influential. Would he seize upon the present situation as his opportunity to rally his dusky braves under the old standard and lead them back along those free, familiar trails which ever led to scenes of plunder and bloodshed? These and similar considerations had determined me not to go upon their reservation until I was prepared to dictate terms to *them* and not they to me; to have the settlers protected in case of open hostilities; and prepared to quell an outbreak without a protracted Indian war.

That General Kautz and his staff were apprehensive of danger was evidenced by the general's action in tendering me a company of cavalry to serve as my personal escort from Tucson to the Chiricahua Agency, which was located in the heart of Apache Pass. As I felt secure with my bodyguard of Apache police, I thanked the general for his consideration and declined the cavalry escort.

It was in the afternoon of June 4, 1876, when I arrived with my Indian police at Sulphur Springs, the scene of Pi-on-se-nay's recent murders. At the same time several companies of cavalry were moving down the Sulphur Springs and San Simon valleys to convenient positions where they might be ready for prompt action in case the renegades attempted further depredations. These two valleys were broad and open so that the approach of the invading forces (each separate column trailed by a dense cloud of dust) could be readily observed by the Chiricahuas, who from adjacent peaks had been watching our movements with the deepest interest.

The crisis for the Chiricahuas had arrived. The next morning the San Carlos police would be at their agency, in the very heart of the pass, with all the supporting troops in position for immediate and effective action. The fighting spirit of Skin-yea, the old war-chief, was thoroughly aroused, and he exerted himself to the utmost in an effort to induce the entire tribe to take the warpath and resist to the bitter end. In this course he was ably supported by his brother, Pi-on-se-nay. Tah-zay and Nah-chee stoutly opposed the plans of the old war-chief. That night the Indians gathered for a council. Suddenly the sharp crack of a rifle rang down the mountain side and the fierce Apache yell proclaimed that deadly strife had begun. Presently, a well directed shot from Nah-chee's gun struck Skin-yea square in the forehead. Scarcely had Pi-on-se-nay realized his brother's death when he was himself completely disabled by a bullet fired by Tah-zay which crashed through his right shoulder. Wounded, defeated, and disheartened, Pi-on-se-nay fled into the shelter of the darkness, assisted by a few of his followers.

Two companies of the Sixth Cavalry en route to Fort Bowie made their camp near mine at Sulphur Springs on the night of

Naiche and his wife, Ha-o-zinne. Naiche was a son of Cochise. Photo taken by A. Frank Randall in 1884. Arizona Historical Society, Tucson, #25635.

June 4. Included among the officers with these troops was Colonel [*James*] Oakes, commander of the regiment. Sulphur Springs was located on the old Southern Overland Stage Route, and the distance to Fort Bowie (in Apache Pass) was twenty-six miles. For about twelve miles the highway led through the open country to the mountains at the mouth of the pass. Inasmuch as my police were marching on foot and the weather was exceedingly warm, I directed them to leave camp at daybreak, in order that they might escape from the valley before the heat became too oppressive, and to wait for me at the mouth of the pass.

Colonel Oakes was traveling in an ambulance with four mules, while I had a light wagon and was driving four light horses. The colonel and I rolled out of camp just as the buglers sounded "boots and saddles" for the troops. Having the lighter and speedier outfit, I reached the mouth of the pass a mile or two in advance of the colonel. My police had arrived an hour before and were well rested. A great cloud of alkali dust down the valley indicated that the troops were plodding along some three or four miles behind their colonel.

When the military ambulance drew up at the mouth of the pass, I asked Colonel Oakes if he intended to await the arrival of his cavalry escort before entering the pass. His response was, "Do you intend to wait for the troops?" I am sure he knew I had no such intention. Anyhow, Colonel Oakes was a "regular fellow" and we were good friends, so I told him that my escort was only awaiting my orders to resume the march. The colonel smiled and said: "Well, Clum, if these police can escort you through the pass they can escort me also, and I'll go right along with you." I assured Colonel Oakes that I would esteem it both a pleasure and an honor to share my escort with him. Thereupon the order was given to proceed.

A dozen alert scouts were detailed as the advance guard and these scattered out along the slopes on either side of the pass to watch for "Indian signs" and to forestall a possible ambush, while the main body of the police were divided into front and rear guards for the two conveyances which were transporting the grizzled colonel and myself. Our progress was cautious but genuinely interesting, tinged with a weird fascination which was not marred by any overt act on the part of the Chiricahuas, and we arrived at Fort Bowie safely, an hour in advance of the colonel's cavalry.

The Chiricahua Agency was located about a mile west from Fort Bowie, and when I arrived there at noon on June 5, 1876, I found both Tah-zay and Nah-chee, the young sons of Cochise (heroes now after their successful fight with the old war-chiefs), were there to greet me, and as soon as I had explained to them fully the purpose of my visit they readily consented to the proposed removal of their band to the San Carlos Reservation.

At this time Agent Jeffords informed me that there was another band of Indians on the reservation known as "Southern Chiricahuas;" that these Indians really belonged in Mexico, but when Cochise made the treaty with General Howard the Southern Chiricahuas elected to include themselves in that treaty and ever since had been reporting quite regularly at the agency for their rations; that the recognized chiefs of this band were Eronemo (Geronimo), Hoo [*Juh*], and Nol-gee; and that these chiefs desired to have an interview with me.

Although I had been actively associated with the affairs of the Arizona Apaches for two years, I had never before heard of Geronimo, and my first meeting with the Indian occurred on the afternoon of June 8, 1876. Accompanied by Hoo and Nol-gee, he related to me how he and his people had joined in the Howard treaty, and now that the young chiefs were going to San Carlos the Southern Chiricahuas desired to go there also. His families, however, were some twenty miles distant, down near the Mexican line, and he only desired permission to go and bring them in. Although this permission was finally granted, the general demeanor of the wily savage did not inspire complete confidence, and, accordingly, some of my scouts were dispatched to shadow his movements.

Geronimo hastened to rejoin his followers, who, in fact, were then located only about ten miles distant from Apache Pass. A few brief orders were quickly given and at once the quiet camp was transformed into a scene of active but cautious preparations for a rapid march. Every bit of superfluous equipage was cast aside. The feeble and disabled horses were killed, as well as the dogs— lest their bark should betray the secret camps of the fleeing savages. As soon as these preparations had been completed the Southern Chiricahuas, with Geronimo in command, moved rapidly to the Mexican line and thence to the Sierra Madre, their former home and which for years after became the stronghold of the renegades.

As soon as my scouts discovered the abandoned camp of the renegades, with its many evidences of a hasty flight, they lost no time in reporting the same to me. Immediately I conveyed this information to General Kautz commanding the Department of

Tom Jeffords (1832-1914). Huntington Library, San Marino, California.

Arizona, who was then at Fort Bowie, and requested him to send some troops to bring back or punish the fleeing Indians. Major [*Albert P.*] Morrow, who, with three companies of cavalry and a company of Indian scouts was stationed in the San Simon Valley just east of Apache Pass, was ordered in pursuit, and although he took up the trail immediately and followed rapidly into Mexico, Geronimo succeeded in making good his escape with all his families and effects.

These events introduced Geronimo to the country as a renegade. Prior to this time he was positively unknown either as "Eronemo," "Heronemo" or "Geronimo" outside the limits of the Chiricahua Reservation and his native haunts in Sonora. He was a full-blooded Apache and Agent Jeffords is authority for the assertion that he was born near Janos, Mexico. [*Janos is a town in northwestern Chihuahua. While Geronimo's band ranged as far south as Janos and beyond, modern historians believe he was born in what is now the United States, near the place where the Gila River crosses the present Arizona-New Mexico line. Geronimo was about fifty-three years old when Clum first met him.*[4]]

During the evening of June 8, a very dark, mean looking Indian came into the agency and announced that he was a member of Pi-on-se-nay's party; that his chief was badly wounded and desired to know upon what terms he might surrender to me. I told him that Pi-on-se-nay was a murderer and would be treated as such, whereupon the messenger expressed the opinion that his chief would not surrender. At once I summoned Tau-el-cly-ee, my sergeant of police, and instructed him to select twenty of his best men and bring in Pi-on-se-nay—alive *if convenient*. At the same time I cautioned him to march with loaded rifles in order that if there was to be any shooting his men would be able to join in the fray with disconcerting alacrity and deadly effect. Then, pointing to the messenger, I said: "This man has just come from Pi-on-se-nay's camp. He will go with you. If he proves a good guide, bring him back, but if not—well, then I don't care to see him again." The sergeant simply grinned and said: "She-bu-ken-see." (I understand.) I then took a Winchester rifle and a six-shooter from the messenger and told him that *if* he came back I would return his arms to him. He did and I did.

Late the next afternoon Tau-el-cly-ee returned bringing with him Pi-on-se-nay and thirty-eight other prisoners—mostly women and children. Tah-zay's bullet had made an ugly wound in Pi-on-se-nay's right shoulder. This wound was carefully dressed daily

Fort Bowie in 1886. Arizona Historical Society, Tucson, #1242.

by the post surgeon at Fort Bowie, and in the meantime my police mounted a double guard over the dangerous prisoner.

Inasmuch as Pi-on-se-nay had been at large over two months since the killing of Rogers and Spence, the citizens of the territory were extremely anxious to know what might be transpiring at Apache Pass. Therefore I wired Governor [*Anson P. K.*] Safford brief details of the murderer's arrest, and also informed him that it was my purpose to bring Pi-on-se-nay to Tucson for confinement and speedy trial in the federal courts. Within a few days I had good reason for regretting that I had advised the governor of my plan to bring the prisoner to Tucson.

Arrangements for the removal were speedily completed; a freight train of "prairie schooners" operated by the firm of Barnett & Block was in readiness for the transportation of baggage and invalids, and on June 12 the sons of Cochise, with their followers, families, and effects, left Apache Pass and started for the San Carlos Reservation without protest. The company totaled 325 men, women, and children, escorted by my Indian police.

As soon as I had seen this picturesque caravan well on its way out of Apache Pass, I returned to the agency for the prisoner, who had been left in the sole custody of that most dependable aide—

Sergeant Tau-el-cly-ee. For my personal transportation I was using a single seated rig and four horses. Placing Pi-on-se-nay on the seat beside me I directed Tau-el-cly-ee to follow close behind, mounted on his faithful steed. Within a couple of hours we had rejoined the caravan, which had struck camp for the night at Ewell Springs in the foothills of the Dos Cabezas range.

As a striking type of the genuine Apache war-chief, Pi-on-se-nay towered as if created for the part. He was a trifle over six feet tall, straight as an arrow, lithe as a panther. His form was that of an ideal athlete; a frame of iron compactly bound with sinews of steel indicating strength, speed, and endurance; clean-cut features as if chiseled by a sculptor; an eye as keen but less friendly than that of Geronimo; and a complexion almost black. Although he was nursing a serious wound during the time he was in my custody, he impressed me as being an Indian who could give a splendid account of himself in any combat, and one whom I would rather not meet alone on the trail if he were in an unfriendly mood.

Because of the apparent painful nature of his wound no shackles had been placed on Pi-on-se-nay. Nevertheless, Tau-el-cly-ee and I were inclined to take every reasonable precaution against the possible escape of our wily and dangerous prisoner during the night. Accordingly, we spread a pair of blankets on the ground, and having allowed Pi-on-se-nay to make himself as comfortable as possible in the center of these, we spread a single blanket over the wounded Indian, weighing down the overlapping ends of this blanket with our own precious bodies as we stretched out for the night on the opposite sides of the prisoner. If we slept at all it was with one eye open, as the saying goes.

June 13 proved to be a very hot day as well as an unlucky day, so far as my plans for Pi-on-se-nay were concerned. The main caravan was in motion at daybreak, for the next camping grounds with water was at Point-of-Mountain Stage Station, thirty miles distant across the Sulphur Springs Valley with its long stretches of alkali shimmering under the blaze of the June sun. Having seen the last of the Chiricahuas on their way, I harnessed-up my four-in-hand [*team of horses*], adjusted Pi-on-se-nay on the seat beside me, and headed westward, with Tau-el-cly-ee and his sturdy charger bringing up the rear.

The duties and responsibilities of the last week had proved a test of endurance, and after a dozen or more miles in the June heat and alkali dust I became a bit drowsy and, for an instant, my eyes closed. When I opened them my dark-visaged companion was glaring at me. Without appearing to heed his gaze, I purposely allowed my head to nod a couple of times and closed my eyes again. When I suddenly aroused myself an instant later my friend the Indian had straightened up his stately form, turned in his seat until he was facing me, and his flashing eyes bespoke the intense excitement he strove to control. He had no weapons. Was he hoping for a chance to snatch one from my belt—my knife—my six-shooter? I don't know. Anyhow, these considerations served to keep me wide awake until we drew rein in front of Tom Williams' road-house at Point-of-Mountain.

Among the first to greet me at this station was Deputy [*Pima County*] Sheriff Charlie Shibell and his assistant, Ad Linn, armed with a warrant for Pi-on-se-nay. [*William S. Oury was sheriff of Pima County. Charles Shibell would replace Oury as sheriff in January 1877.*[5]] I had planned to convey the prisoner to Tucson personally, with a guard of Indian police, but the deputy sheriffs, with the warrant, held the right-of-way. So I delivered Pi-on-se-nay into their custody about two o'clock p.m. on that thirteenth day of June, and at nine o'clock that same evening the old war-chief escaped. This, of course, was a great misfortune, as the trial and punishment of this murderer, under the direction of the federal courts, would have had a most beneficial and far-reaching influence among the Apaches of Arizona. And what grieved me more was the firm conviction that if Pi-on-se-nay had remained in my custody, the Indian police would have landed him in the jail at Tucson not later than June 15, 1876. Pi-on-se-nay was killed in Mexico about two years later.

The following is quoted from my annual report for 1876 to the Commissioner of Indian Affairs: "On June 18 the Chiricahua Indians were located on the San Carlos Reservation without trouble or accident. The terrible shade of that tribe's dreaded name had passed away, and the imaginary army of four or five hundred formidable warriors had dwindled to the modest number of sixty half-armed and less clothed savages."

In the fall of 1876 I took a score of Apaches, including Tah-zay, on a trip to the East. While visiting at Washington, Tah-zay was stricken with pneumonia and died. He is buried in the Congressional Cemetery, where his ashes rest amid the graves of many other distinguished Americans. General O. O. Howard, who made the treaty with Tah-zay's father four years prior, attended the funeral.

◇ ◇ ◇ ◇ ◇

With the removal of the Cochise Indians to San Carlos the Chiricahua Reservation was abandoned, hence it was no longer convenient for Geronimo and his band to step from Mexico onto the reservation and again from the reservation back into Mexico. While this was a decided handicap to the renegades it did not deter them from making frequent raids through southeastern Arizona and across into southwestern New Mexico, where they had friends among the former followers of old Mangas Colorado, one of whom was Ponce, who accompanied General Howard into Cochise's stronghold [*in 1872*]. Troops were frequently sent out for the purpose of intercepting and punishing these marauding bands, but Geronimo succeeded in evading pursuit until the San Carlos police were again ordered on his trail.

The dissatisfaction of the people of Arizona with the inadequate protection afforded settlers in the southeastern part of the territory by the military and the ineffectual efforts of the troops to apprehend and punish the bands of renegade Apaches who were making too frequent raids from Sonora and New Mexico was expressed in no uncertain terms by the territorial legislature. On February 8, 1877, that body passed an appro-priation of $10,000 and authorized the governor to enroll sixty militia for the protection of citizens against hostile Indians. [*In January 1877 Arizona's ninth territorial legislature convened in Tucson, but it was the last time the lawmakers met there—the capital was moved from Tucson to Prescott later that year.*]

Immediately Governor Safford wired me a request for sixty of my San Carlos police to serve as territorial militia against the renegades. I advised the governor that I would be happy to comply with his request provided Captain [*Clay*] Beauford, my chief of police, could be placed in charge of this militia company, as I did not deem it wise to send these Apache police out under the command of a stranger. Governor Safford promptly gave his hearty approval to my suggestion. On February 20th I arrived in Tucson with this company of police and turned them over to the governor. Without delay Captain Beauford and the Indians were enrolled as territorial militia, equipped and rationed, and on February 23rd were dispatched for active scouting in southeastern Arizona.

My school days included a three-years' course at a military academy, and during the last two years at that institution I held the rank of captain. This, of course, made me familiar with the manual of arms and company drill, and as we had four companies

Anson P. K. Safford (1828-1891) served as Arizona's governor from 1869 to 1877. He, like John Clum, often criticized General Kautz and his handling of Apache unrest. Arizona Historical Society, Tucson, #13757.

we frequently indulged in skirmish and battalion drills. Because of my fondness for military maneuvers I had amused myself sometimes by drilling my Indian police. A pleasing result of this pastime is shown in a photograph of my bodyguard taken at Tucson in May 1876, in which the company is formed in a "column of twos."

The transfer of a body of Apache police to the governor of Arizona for service as territorial militia in a campaign against hostile Indians was a unique event in frontier history. Such a momentous occasion seemed to demand some elaborate and spectacular ceremony, and nothing could be more appropriate than a military gesture, with the firing of a salute by the entire company as a climax. The Apache police had never heard of blank cartridges and therefore it seemed to them entirely proper that ball cartridges should be used in firing the salute, in which opinion I heartily concurred inasmuch as no blanks were obtainable. The trail from San Carlos to Tucson measured about 125 miles, and short drills were held each morning and evening while en route. As the Indians entered heartily into the spirit of the game we were able to make a very creditable showing when the fateful moment arrived for our grand act.

On reaching Tucson I marched the company in a column of twos to the "Governor's Palace." [*Governor Safford's residence in adobe Tucson was a far cry from a palace.*] Here the company was halted and stood at parade rest, facing the palace, while I rapped at the door. As soon as the governor appeared the company was brought to attention. Orders were then given for the following evolutions: "Carry Arms;" "Rear Open Order;" "About Face;"

"Load;" "Aim;" "Fire;" "Recover Arms;" "About Face;" "Close Order;" "Present Arms." These orders were given in English and the evolutions followed the old Upton tactics. Having fired the salute and with the company standing at "present," I made my most graceful personal salutation to the governor and "delivered the goods." The following local item appeared in the *Arizona Citizen* (Tucson), Saturday, February 24, 1877:

> Indian Agent John P. Clum arrived here on Tuesday with sixty stalwart armed Apaches from San Carlos Reservation, with a view to their enlistment under the call of the governor in pursuance of an act of the late legislature. Mr. Clum marched them in front of the governor's office where they fired a salute and were inspected by the governor. Afterward they were assigned Tully, Ochoa & Co.'s large corral as a camping ground where they remained until leaving for the field Friday. Their conduct was orderly and highly creditable in every way. Captain Beauford informed us that he did not even have to speak to any of them in a corrective tone. Agent Clum in this instance has done the public a very valuable service and given another of many proofs of his desire to promote the welfare of the people generally.

Meanwhile there were reports of frequent raids in which stock was stolen and traded off at the small towns along the Rio Grande, thus adding much to the prosperity of the renegades. It so happened that Lieutenant Henely, who led the troops from [*Fort*] Bowie on the trail of Pi-on-se-nay in April 1876, was passing through the Rio Grande valley in the latter part of February 1877. There he saw Geronimo, whither he had come on one of his "trading" tours. Lieut. Henely at once telegraphed to General Kautz that he had seen Geronimo in the vicinity of Las Palomas [*near present-day Truth or Consequences*] and that the renegade undoubtedly was making his headquarters at the Southern Apache Agency at Ojo Caliente, New Mexico. [*The Ojo Caliente (Warm Springs) Reservation was located about twenty miles northwest of Las Palomas on the Rio Alamosa. It was headquarters for the Eastern Chiricahua band led by Victorio.*[6]] General Kautz telegraphed this information to the War Department, and that department transmitted the facts to the commissioner of Indian affairs. The result was the following telegram to me:

Washington, D.C.,
March 20, 1877.

Agent Clum, San Carlos:

If practicable take Indian police and arrest renegade Indians at Southern Apache Agency; seize stolen horses in their possession, restore property to rightful owners, remove renegades to San Carlos and hold them in confinement for murder and robbery. Call on military for aid if needed.

Smith, Commissioner.

These orders imposed upon me one of the most important and exciting campaigns I have ever undertaken. With the approval of Governor Safford, I sent a courier to Captain Beauford directing him to proceed at once to Silver City, N.M., with his company, and, having enrolled about forty additional police at San Carlos, I hastened to join Beauford at Silver City. At that point the "Arizona Apache Territorial Militia" was taken over by me and their names once more entered upon the agency pay roll, Captain Beauford included. Having thus been reinstated as members of the San Carlos Indian Police Force they were merged with the company I had brought from San Carlos, and the entire body proceeded thenceforth under my direction. The distance by trail from San Carlos to Ojo Caliente is something like 350 or 400 miles, and the greater part of my little army of Indians measured the entire distance of the round trip on foot.

General [*Edward*] Hatch was in command of the Department of New Mexico with headquarters at Santa Fe. Just before leaving San Carlos I sent a despatch to General Hatch advising him of the nature of my orders and requesting him to assign sufficient troops at convenient stations in the field to co-operate in the protection of the citizens of southwestern New Mexico should serious trouble occur. At Fort Bayard [*near Silver City*] I received a reply from General Hatch informing me that in compliance with my request he had ordered eight companies of the Ninth Cavalry into the field. Having completed all preliminary details, I left Silver City with my police and started on the long trek over the mountains to Ojo Caliente. All along the route we were warned that the main body of the renegades was gathered in the vicinity of the Southern

Welford Bridwell (1846-1905) took the name Clay Beauford when he joined the Confederate Army as an underage youth. He returned to using the name Bridwell in 1879. John P. Clum Collection, Special Collections Department, University of Arizona Library.

Apache Agency, that this aggregation totaled from 250 to 400 well armed, desperate Indians, and that these rude and ruthless redskins were impatiently waiting for an opportunity to greet us in the most enthusiastic fashion. These rumors served to sustain the interest in our march into New Mexico.

At Fort Bayard it had been arranged that Major [*James F.*] Wade, commanding the troops in the field and who was then at Fort Union, should meet me at Ojo Caliente with three companies of cavalry on the morning of April 21st, but when I arrived at that point on the evening of April 20th I found there a telegram from Major Wade advising me that he would not be able to reach Ojo Caliente until April 22nd. Doubtless this delay was unavoidable, but it placed the full responsibility of a most serious situation squarely up to me. It was obvious that if I remained two days at Ojo Caliente with my San Carlos police there would not be a renegade within fifty miles of that point. But troops were now co-operating at my request. If I took any action against the renegades without consulting the officer commanding the troops in the field, I must be solely responsible for the results.

I had sent a dependable scout to Ojo Caliente several days in advance of my arrival, and he informed me that Geronimo, with between 80 and 100 followers, was then camped about three miles from the agency and that he had come in to the agency that very day for rations. We had been on the trail nearly a month and had marched all the way from San Carlos for the special purpose of arresting Geronimo. Our only chance for success was through prompt and resolute action. In these circumstances I determined that we would undertake to make the arrest without delay, relying entirely upon the loyalty and efficiency of the Apache police.

As before stated, most of my police were on foot. We had marched cautiously to within twenty miles of the agency, where we had camped at noon on April 20th. There I selected the twenty-two Apache scouts who had horses as a special body-guard to accompany me to the agency, where we arrived shortly before sundown. Captain Beauford was instructed to bring the main body of the police to a spring about ten miles from the agency that evening and to complete the march to the agency leisurely the following morning. This proved a most fortunate maneuver. The renegades knew that some Indian police were on the trail from Arizona, but they did not know how many, and their general attitude after my arrival at the agency convinced me that they were of the opinion that the twenty-two police who escorted me in constituted my entire force. Upon this hypothesis I based my plan of action.

The main agency building faced the east, fronting on a large parade ground. About fifty yards to the south stood a large commissary building which, happily, was vacant. From this commissary building a row of employee quarters extended eastward along the south line of the parade ground, while the east and north limits of the parade ground were marked by a deep ravine. Such was the general plan of the field on which I hoped the renegades might speedily be lured to their "Waterloo."

As soon as it was dark I dispatched a courier to Captain Beauford with orders to bring his reserves in before daylight and to observe the utmost caution and quiet in approaching the agency. At about 4 a.m. the reserves, numbering about eighty, arrived and were at once quartered in the convenient commissary building, each man with thirty rounds of fixed ammunition and his gun loaded. This bit of stratagem, in which the innocent commissary building was destined to duplicate the trick of the famous Trojan Horse, operated so effectively that it has been a matter of self-congratulation ever since.

At daylight I sent a messenger to the renegade camp to inform Geronimo and the other chiefs that I desired to have a "talk" with them. They came quickly—a motley clan painted and equipped for a fight. Supported by a half-dozen of my police I took my position on the porch of the main agency building overlooking the parade ground. The remainder of my special escort of twenty-two were deployed in an irregular skirmish line, half of them northward toward the ravine and the other half southward to the commissary building. Captain Beauford had his station halfway between me and the commissary, and, let me repeat, every man had thirty rounds of fixed ammunition and his gun loaded.

The police were instructed to be constantly on the alert and ready for instant combat, but not to shoot: (1) unless ordered to do so by either Captain Beauford or myself; (2) unless Captain Beauford or I began shooting; (3) unless the renegades began shooting. The reserves were instructed that at a signal from Captain Beauford their sergeant would swing wide the great commissary doors and then race eastward along the south line of the parade ground, and they were to follow hot on his trail at intervals of about two paces, every man with his thumb on the hammer of his gun.

Because the renegades believed they held a decided advantage in the matter of numbers, I did not think they would hesitate to assemble on the parade ground in front of my position, and this proved true. They came trailing in just as the sun rose gloriously above the New Mexican ranges. Was this to be the final sunrise for some, or many, of us who were watching it—and each other—so anxiously?

Sullen and defiant, the renegades were finally gathered in a fairly compact group in front of me, and, as is their custom on such occasions, their most daring men (and just the men I wanted, such as Geronimo, Gordo, Ponce, Francisco, etc.) were pressed forward as a menace to my personal safety. They fully appreciated that the immediate presence of such desperate characters, fully armed and smeared with paint, is anything but reassuring to a "paleface."

Promptly I addressed my exceedingly picturesque audience, telling them that I had come a long distance on a very important mission, but if they would listen to my words "with good ears" no serious harm would be done to them. With equal promptness Geronimo replied that if I spoke with discretion no serious harm would be done to us, or words to that effect. This defiant attitude convinced me that it would be useless to continue the parley. The crisis had arrived. The hour had struck which was to determine the success or failure of our expedition. The excitement, though suppressed, was keen. Would they, upon discovering our superior force and arms, submit without a struggle, or would the next moment precipitate a hand-to-hand fight to the death between these desperate renegades and the bravest and best fighters the Apache tribes of Arizona could produce? On either side were the most determined of men. The slightest cause might change the history of the day.

The situation demanded action—*prompt action*—and very promptly the signal was given. Instantly the commissary portals swung open and Sergeant Rip started his sprint along the south line of the parade grounds. As if by magic the reserves came swarming out from the commissary, and, in single file, leaped after the sergeant at top speed with intervals that left room for the free use of their weapons. We had started the action—most impressive and spectacular action—with those lithe Apache police bounding along, each with his thumb on the hammer of his loaded rifle, alert, ready, and, thus far, in comparative silence.

However, the release of the reserves had not failed to startle the renegades. At the same time there was enacted a little side-play which, in my judgement, was potent in deciding the issues of the day. At the first sight of the reserves emerging from the old commissary building, a half-dozen of the straggling followers of the hostiles started to move away from the parade ground. When these failed to obey our orders to return, Captain Beauford raised his rifle and leveled it at one of the would-be fugitives. There are always a few belligerent squaws who insist upon intruding whenever a "war-talk" is in progress and one of these athletic ladies had stationed herself, doubtless designedly, close by our stalwart chief of police. With a wild yell she sprang upon Beauford and clung to his neck and arms in such a manner as to draw down his rifle, making a superb "tackle" and "interference." I had been keeping my two eyes on Geronimo, but with the echo of that genuine Apache yell I turned just in time to appreciate Beauford's expression of profound disgust when he discovered that he had been captured by a squaw. Then he swung that great right arm to which the lady was clinging and she landed ingloriously on the parade ground and at a respectful distance. Really, a bit of comedy injected into a most serious situation.

This episode consumed less that a minute, but it held the attention of the entire audience and enabled us to get fifteen or twenty additional police in that galloping skirmish line. Also, when Captain Beauford raised his gun the second time the police indicated that they were ready to follow his lead if shooting was to become general. All of which produced a most wholesome effect on the minds of the renegades. In the meantime, the maneuver of the reserves was such a complete surprise and had been executed with such dash and daring that before the renegades fully realized what was happening they found themselves at the mercy of a threatened cross fire from our two skirmish lines, which were now deployed on the west and south sides of the parade grounds, with the angle at the old commissary building. Geronimo was quick to comprehend the hopelessness of his position. Thereupon he recalled the stragglers and readily agreed to a conference.

Immediately I directed Geronimo and three or four of his lieutenants to come to the porch where I was standing. Their compliance was stoical. Feeling assured that the crucial moment had passed, I handed my rifle to one of my police and told Geronimo that as we were to have a "peace talk" we would both lay aside our arms. Geronimo frowned his objection, but we had the advantage. I took his gun from him, a bit rudely perhaps, and the same is still in my possession, a much prized trophy of that expedition. [*This rifle is now owned by the Arizona Historical Society.*]

Having taken the guns from a half a dozen other "bad" men we settled down for a peace talk. Geronimo adjusted himself in a

This "trap door" Springfield Model 1870 rifle, caliber .50-70, was taken from Geronimo by John Clum and his policemen in April 1877. The weapon had been shortened to carbine length. It was acquired from the Clum family by the Arizona Historical Society in 1976.

squatting position on the porch immediately in front of me. I began by reminding him that we had met nearly a year before at Apache Pass when he had agreed to accompany the Chiricahua Indians to San Carlos. To this he replied, "Yes, and you gave me a pass to go out and bring in my people, but I could not get back within the time you allowed, so I did not return—I was afraid." In a most serious manner I told him the story of the killing of his dogs and old horses; his deserted camp; his hasty march into Sonora; the pursuit of the troops, etc., and suggested that if he had really desired to go to San Carlos he would not have hot-footed it in the opposite direction. He gave me a fierce glance but made no reply. "Well," I continued, "I must be your good friend because I have traveled so far to see you again. Now I want to keep you with me and to know where you are, and so I will provide you with a special escort and then you will not stray away and be afraid to return."

Geronimo glared in sullen silence. Thereupon I ordered him to go with the police to the guardhouse. He did not move. Then I added, "You must go now." Like a flash he leaped to his feet. There was a picture I shall never forget. He stood erect as a mountain pine, while every outline of his symmetrical form indicated strength and endurance. His abundant ebony locks draped his ample shoulders, his stern features, his keen piercing eye, and his proud and graceful posture combined to create in him the model of an Apache war-chief. There he stood, Geronimo the

Renegade, a form commanding admiration, a name and character dreaded by all. His eyes blazed fiercely under the excitement of the moment and his form quivered with a suppressed rage. From his demeanor it was evident to all that he was hesitating between two purposes—whether to draw his knife, his only remaining weapon, and cut right and left and die fighting, or to surrender.

My police were not slow in discerning the thoughts of the renegade. Instantly Sergeant Rip sprang forward and snatched the knife from Geronimo's belt, while the muzzles of a half-dozen guns in the hands of Beauford and the police were pressed toward him, their locks clicking almost in unison as the hammers were drawn back. With flashing eyes he permitted himself to indulge in a single swift, defiant glance at his captors. Then his features relaxed and he said calmly, "In-gew" ("All right"), and thus was accomplished the first and only bona fide capture of Geronimo the Renegade. [*Following escapes from San Carlos and periods of liberty in northern Mexico, Geronimo would surrender to U.S. authorities in 1879, 1884, and finally in 1886. But on these occasions he gave up his freedom after lengthy negotiations—he was never again captured at gunpoint.7*] The prisoner was forthwith escorted to the black-smith shop, and thence to the guardhouse. At the blacksmith shop shackles were riveted on the prisoner's ankles. These were never removed while he remained in my custody, and never should have been removed except to allow him to walk untrammeled to the scaffold.

Immediately following the arrest of Geronimo six other renegades were taken into custody, disarmed and shackled, one of whom was Ponce. But at that time I had no idea I was arresting an Indian who had been a trusted and useful member of General Howard's official party on his important mission to Cochise's Stronghold [*in 1872*]. While en route over the mountains from Silver City to Ojo Caliente we had cut the hot trail of a raiding band which my scouts found led back to the Warm Springs Reservation. After my arrival at the agency I learned that this band had preceded us there only a couple of days; that they had brought in some stolen stock; that Ponce was the leader of this band; and that he exerted a great influence among the renegades. This was all I knew of Ponce, and it was on this record that I caused his arrest.

And thus it transpired that when Major Wade finally arrived at Ojo Caliente with his escort of cavalry on April 22nd, Geronimo and the other principal renegades had been arrested and shackled and were under guard by the San Carlos police.

My orders from Washington under date of March 20th having been successfully executed, it was decided that Captain Beauford with the main body of police should start on their return march to Arizona without delay with the hope of intercepting some small bands of renegades who were believed to be raiding between Ojo Caliente and the Dos Cabezas Mountains. Accordingly, I selected twenty-five of the police to serve as my personal escort and guard for the prisoners and furnished the remainder with thirty-days' rations and 3,000 rounds of ammunition. Thus equipped and in high spirits Captain Beauford and his command took the homeward-bound trail on the morning of April 23rd.

About this time I received a telegram from the Commissioner of Indian Affairs directing me to take all of the Indians at the Warm Springs Agency to San Carlos "if, upon consultation with the military authorities, such action was deemed desirable." General Hatch and his staff heartily favored the proposed removal and arrangements were at once made to that effect. Victorio, who later became notorious as a desperate renegade, was the recognized chief of the Warm Springs Indians [*the Eastern Chiricahua band*] at that time, and neither he nor any of his followers made serious objection to the removal after they had learned from me and my police force the manner in which all Indians were cared for at San Carlos. As these Indians had very few household effects, and a majority of them had been living under conditions which made it necessary for them to be ready to move at a moment's notice, all preparations for the march to San Carlos were quickly concluded.

General Hatch had not only been cordial in his co-operation but had been most generous in his commendations of the splendid results accomplished by the San Carlos Apache police. In these circumstances I felt it would be courteous to request him to detail a small escort of cavalry to accompany the main body of the Warm Springs Indians over the trail to San Carlos. I even argued that such an escort was desirable owing to the fact that Captain Beauford and his command were well on their way to Silver City before the order for this removal was received, therefore no police were available to serve as an escort. General Hatch was both cheerful and prompt in complying with my request. Lieutenant [*William H.*] Hugo and a few troopers were detailed for this duty.

May 1, 1877, was the date set for our departure from Ojo Caliente and all seemed in readiness for the start to Arizona. But on that morning, while hurrying about to assure myself that all were actually on the move, I saw an Indian sitting on a step in front of one of the employee quarters, his elbows on his knees, his face in his hands, and his loose hair covering both face and hands. When I spoke to him he simply moaned. Very soon I discovered that this Indian had smallpox. The situation was desperate. We must start on the return trip. This Indian could not travel with the others, and I could not leave him alone to die. Fortunately, one of my policemen had had the disease and was immune. He consented to drive the team assigned to convey the sick Indian in a hastily improvised ambulance. In less than an hour after I first saw the sick Indian his transportation had been provided and he had joined our caravan—however, always maintaining a respectful distance in the rear of the wagon conveying the prisoners.

Mr. M. A. Sweeney, chief clerk at the San Carlos agency, who had preceded me to Ojo Caliente on scout duty, was given full charge of the main body of the Indians on this march over the mountains to Silver City. An actual count showed 453 men, women, and children. This company presented a very long and very thin line as they stretched out along the trail, and at the end of this line followed Lieutenant Hugo and his guard of honor. I have mentioned this "very long and very thin line" and the "guard of honor" for the purpose of correcting the statement that these Indians were "transported forcibly" from Ojo Caliente to San Carlos. Lieutenant Hugo was a capable officer and a good fellow and he led willing troopers, but it was obviously impossible for him to patrol effectively that very long and very thin line with thirty or forty soldiers, and if any of those Indians had determined to scatter into the mountains he could not have prevented their going, nor could he have effected their capture with his limited command. The difficulty experienced by troops in their efforts to apprehend and punish fleeing or marauding bands of Indians has been demonstrated too frequently. Moreover, Mr. Sweeney informed me that during this march a majority of the Indians were from ten to twenty miles in advance of this "guard." Even if Captain Beauford and his San Carlos police had been patrolling the trail, these could hardly have prevented the escape of small parties had any of the Warm Springs Indians entertained determined opposition to removal to San Carlos.

Having seen the main body of the Indians started on the westward trail, and having arranged for the transportation of the sick Indian by means of the improvised "portable isolation hospital," I could now give my undivided attention to the prisoners. The shackles which the prisoners were wearing were homemade and were riveted to the ankles. This made it impracticable to convey them over the trail, as they could neither walk nor ride on horseback. Therefore, a large transport wagon was provided for their accommodation, into which they were loaded as comfortably as circumstances would permit. Our provisions and camp outfit were carried in another wagon, and at a safe distance behind these two vehicles trailed our "peripatetic pesthouse." The special escort of police, all well mounted, were divided into squads—advance and rear guards—and with my last duty at Ojo Caliente accomplished I mounted my horse, waved a signal which meant "Let's go," and the tedious trek to San Carlos was begun.

Although homeward bound, the first stage of our journey led us further away from Arizona. In order to pass a spur of the mountains which extend southeasterly from Ojo Caliente it was necessary to follow the wagon road back to Las Palomas on the Rio Grande; thence southwesterly to old Fort Cummings; and thence northwesterly to Silver City where we joined the main body of the Indians who had come over the [*foot*] trail. From Silver City we proceeded westerly over the Burro Mountains and thence to the Gila valley which was followed to the San Carlos Reservation.

The smallpox developed into a really serious situation, as the disease was then prevalent in both New Mexico and Arizona. [*In 1877 smallpox killed some two hundred people in Tucson and hundreds more in other parts of the territory.*[8]] After we left Silver City our ambulatory hospital was taxed to the limit and several died on the trail. Even after the Indians had been located at their new home on the Gila, the malady continued to manifest itself with more or less fatal results. Barring the ravages of this disease, the removal of the Warm Springs Indians was accomplished without serious difficulty or mishap. The prisoners gave us no trouble en route and on May 20 were safely delivered into the agency guardhouse at San Carlos.

The efficiency of the San Carlos Indian police force once more had been demonstrated in a conspicuous manner. During the round trip the police had traveled approximately 800 miles. A majority of them had covered the entire distance on foot. Unaided by the troops, they had accomplished the arrest of Geronimo and sixteen other outlaw Indians. Twenty-five members of this force were detailed as the sole escort and guard to accompany the renegade prisoners while en route in wagons from Ojo Caliente to San Carlos, a distance by the wagon road of fully 500 miles. The anticipated danger of an organized attack and attempt to rescue

Charles Shibell (1841-1908) served as Pima County sheriff from 1877 to 1880. He and other officials disappointed John Clum by not prosecuting Geronimo for murder. Henry Buehman photo, Arizona Historical Society, Tucson, #6972.

the prisoners by some of their renegade friends who were still at large had not materialized, but the police had been constantly alert, prepared for any emergency. For twenty days and twenty nights they had kept faithful watch and vigil, and when the journey ended they delivered their prisoners safely and in irons to the agency police on duty at the guardhouse at San Carlos. Sure! They finished the job!

My original orders from Washington were to arrest Geronimo and hold him in confinement "for murder and robbery," and I felt that the next step in his career should be a trial in the federal courts. In fact this seemed the only intelligent and just course to pursue. It was obvious that the trial and conviction of this renegade in the regular courts of the "paleface" would produce a tremendously beneficial moral effect upon the Indians generally, and inasmuch as Pi-on-se-nay had cheated us out of such an example less than a year previous, I was especially desirous of bringing Geronimo to trial. Accordingly, I advised the sheriff of Pima County [*Charles Shibell*] at Tucson that Geronimo was held in the guardhouse at San Carlos in irons subject to his orders or the orders of the court he represented, that he was charged with murder and robbery, and that I was anxious to assist in supplying the evidence necessary to secure a conviction. No action was taken by the sheriff and Geronimo was never brought to trial.

Olympic Theatre!

A NOVEL ATTRACTION.

Friday and Saturday Evenings, September 8th & 9th,
And Saturday Matinee,
Only appearances of members of the Famous Indian Tribes of

WILD APACHES

OF ARIZONA.

Under the direction of Mr. J. P. Clum, Ex-Indian Agent,
numbering

Sixteen Stalwart Braves and Four Squaws

Without doubt the Finest Specimen of the Aborigine ever seen
in this city.

The entertainment will consist of a series of

Stirring Tableaux,

Intensely and accurately illustrative of

Indian Modes & Customs

Never before so faithfully set forth.

FIRST TABLEAU.
THE INDIANS IN FULL COSTUMES,
Introductory remarks by Mr. J. P. Clum.

SECOND TABLEAUX.
AN INDIAN ENCAMPMENT,
The Surprise! The Fight! Thrilling Hand-to-Hand
Combat! Taking of the Scalp! Triumph of the Whites!

THIRD TABLEAU.
AN INDIAN COUNCIL OF WAR.
Speeches in the Indian Language by the noted Braves & Chiefs.

FOURTH TABLEAU.
Indian Woman Mourning the Death of her Husband.

FIFTH TABLEAUX.
Grand War Dance. Preparing for the War-Path.

OVERTURE. - - - - ORCHESTRA

PART SECOND—FIRST TABLEAU.
INDIAN TELEGRAPHIC SYSTEM.

SECOND TABLEAUX.
Whites Encamped. The Indian Attack.
Capture of the Hunter. Taking of the Scalp.
Securing the Prisoner to the Stake.
His Torture. Indian Scalp Dance.

THIRD TABLEAUX.
Indian Police Regulations. Arresting a Renegade.

FINAL TABLEAUX.
The Indian at Home, and at Peace.
Squaws engaged in Domestic Labor. Social Scenes. The whole
concluding with A SOCIAL DANCE.

INDIAN MATINEE, SATURDAY
At Reduced Prices, 50 and 25 Cents to all parts of the house.

Monday, Sept. 11th, opening of the Regular Fall and Winter
Season.

Mr. C. W. BARRY
in his New drama, ECHOES.

Geo. E. Ward & Co. Printers, No. 208 North Fourth St., Cincinnati, O.

Handbill advertizing the St. Louis opening of John Clum's "Wild
Apache" show. John P. Clum Collection, Special Collections
Department, University of Arizona Library.

8

APACHES AS THESPIANS

Editor's note: Throughout his life, John Clum was fascinated by the theater and acting. But none of his forays into the world of entertainment was as audacious as the "Wild Apache" show he organized in Arizona and took on the road to the settled Eastern states in 1876. This was the first time that Apaches had been seen east of Texas, and they created a sensation. Out West Apaches were feared by other Indian tribes, White settlers, and Mexican villagers alike, and their reputation was well known in the East. Geronimo, Victorio, Juh, and other warriors were still roaming the hills and preying upon vulnerable trespassers, and stories of their exploits were told far and wide. But young John Clum (he was twenty-five years old) had confidence in his Apache players. He was convinced that the Apache problem was caused by a few incorrigible renegades, such as Geronimo, and by insensitive military officers and unscrupulous White profiteers. Clum had no doubt that if treated with respect most Apaches, like other people, would respond in kind. In this belief John Clum was decades ahead of his time. The following article by Clum was first published in January 1931 in the New Mexico Historical Review.

"Olympic Theatre! A Novel Attraction! Wild Apaches of Arizona! Stirring Tableau! Under the direction of Mr. John P. Clum, Ex-Indian Agent. Friday and Saturday Evenings, September 8th and 9th, and Saturday Matinee." These phrases are excerpts from an announcement by the manager of the Olympic Theatre at Saint Louis, Missouri, for the week ending September 9, 1876.

When I was appointed agent for the Apaches in 1874 they were reputed to be the most desperate, treacherous, and bloodthirsty tribe within the United States. "The Apache is a savage of the lowest type" was the initial sentence in the annual report of 1878 submitted by General August V. Kautz commanding the Department of Arizona. While this and similar contemporaneous pronouncements against the Apaches were unwarranted, nevertheless from a retrospective viewpoint the plan to take a party of these nomadic Indians in 1876 direct from their trails and fastnesses within the (then) remote mountain areas of Arizona and transform them, as if by magic, into valiant actors upon the stages of first class theatres in some of our largest cities to the eastward looms as an exceedingly ambitious and daring undertaking. And yet, while this enterprize was in course of incubation, I well remember that the feature of greatest concern was that of necessary funds to transport our aboriginal theatrical troupe from the isolated trails of Arizona to the great centers of population in the East.

Prior to the adoption of the civil service plan it was doubtless true that the majority of civil government appointees entertained a more or less justifiable fear of being unceremoniously separated from their respective jobs, and the matter of a potent political pull was of paramount importance. My personal status in this particular was at least unique for the reason that, although my political backing was practically nil, during the greater part of the latter half of my administration as Indian Agent at San Carlos my resignation was on file at the office of the Commissioner of Indian Affairs.

There were two principal causes for this unusual situation. In the first place certain weaknesses in the "policy" of the Indian Bureau pertaining to the direction of the affairs of the Apaches persistently discouraged any inclination I might have had to remain permanently in charge at San Carlos. The second and more important reason was that with my resignation on file at Washington I felt entirely free at all times to exercise my best judgement in connection with my duties and responsibilities as agent, conscious of the fact that my superior officers at the Department of the Interior were in a position either to approve my official conduct and methods or promptly to accept my resignation and appoint my successor.

And so it happened that my theatrical venture with the Apaches was a direct sequence of this habit of resigning. My original resignation as agent was submitted on February 27, 1876, just two years subsequent to the date of my appointment. About six weeks later—April 6, 1876—the outbreak of the Chiricahua Apaches occurred. On May 3, instead of being relieved, I received telegraphic orders to remove the Chiricahuas to San Carlos. This important assignment was accomplished during the month of June. Although this removal added 325 individuals to the population of the San Carlos Reservation, we were still happily able to report "all quiet on the western front."

That [*1876*] being the national centennial year, the citizens of

Tucson arranged for a somewhat elaborate celebration on the Fourth of July, and I cheerfully accepted their invitation to be present on that occasion. The Fourth of July celebration passed into history, but no successor for my job had been announced, whereupon there arose in my mind the very pertinent question, "Where do we go from here?"

The idea of taking some of the Apaches on a tour of "the states" was not new with me. For nearly a year I had felt that much good would result if I were allowed to take representatives of the several bands on a trip through our great country to the eastward—at least as far as Washington. In fact, I had applied to the Commissioner of Indian Affairs for authority to make such a trip, but permission was withheld for the reason that no funds were available with which to meet the expenses involved.

However, the proposition had appealed to me so strongly that now, with the added lure of the Centennial Exposition at Philadelphia, I determined not to allow the matter of mere money to stand in our way, particularly as conditions upon the reservation indicated that this was an opportune time for undertaking the trip. My administration was so well organized and the mass of the Apaches were so friendly disposed toward said administration that I felt confident peace and harmony would prevail until the arrival of my successor. Furthermore, if influential members of the several bands accompanied me, these would serve in the nature of hostages pledging the orderly conduct of their people during our absence. In fact, as soon as the leaders among the Apaches displayed their sympathy with, and their interest in, the proposed tour, I did not hesitate to exert myself in making the trip possible.

Our chief handicap was the lack of necessary funds. In this extremity the plan of giving entertainments with the Apaches was suggested. Instantly the enterprise captivated the romantic imaginations and adventurous spirits of two young friends and myself. The appearance of a group of Apaches always attracted a crowd, even in Arizona—provided the Indians were not on the warpath. The ranchers and townsfolk evinced unfeigned curiosity and interest whenever I appeared on the trails or in the villages with an escort of Indians, and less than two months previous [*on May 26, 1876*] fully two-thirds of the entire population of Tucson assembled on the old Military Plaza in that ancient pueblo to witness an Apache war-dance given by members of the company of Apache police then with me en route to Apache Pass.

In view of these circumstances we felt assured that there were thousands of people in the East who would gladly pay a small fee

to obtain a glimpse of the spectacular, picturesque, and wooly-
wild West as portrayed by the only, original, genuine
representatives of the fierce Apaches direct from their mountain
fastnesses in Arizona. All we needed was sufficient funds to
transport our ambulatory Apache aggregation from their crude
wiki-ups in the West to the flashing footlights in the East. We
clearly envisioned vast throngs besieging the theatres where we
were advertised to appear, and ourselves speedily advancing into
the millionaire class as a result of the amazing returns from the
box-offices. Furthermore, we would automatically loom as public
benefactors—philanthropists—for the reason that we would be
affording the Indians the desired benefits of a tour through the
vast camping grounds of the paleface, while contenting ourselves
with the problematical returns from the "gate."

The more we discussed the proposition the more enthusiastic
and optimistic we became. I may state now that the sanguine
mental attitude on the part of my two friends and myself was
largely due to the fact that we were young and robust—and
inexperienced in the show business. Our lack of experience and
caution, from a cold business viewpoint, is illustrated by the fact
that, although a brief announcement of the slaughter of the gallant
Custer and his entire command by the Sioux on June 25th [*1876*]
had reached Arizona, we did not stop to consider the inevitable
reaction of this tragedy at the North [*Montana*] upon the people of
the East, and that in all probability the entire country would be
swept by a wave of extreme prejudice against all of the so-called
"savage" tribes of the West.

After mature deliberation our optimistic trio decided that a
cash capital of $5,000 would be required to place the enterprise
upon a paying basis. One of my friends had some real money
(more dollars than *sense* in this investment) and he was so
confident of the success of the enterprise that he offered to
provide one-half of the necessary capital if the other friend and
myself would dig up the balance. This was done. The die was cast,
and about the middle of July, 1876, I found myself designated as
the manager of a troupe of Apache thespians, backed by a cash
capital of $5,000 with which to carry on until we should reach a
paying basis. The fact that I had not obtained leave of absence for
myself, or permission to remove the Indians so far from their
reservation, did not cause the least hesitation or delay in the
execution of our plans.

Inasmuch as we lacked proper authority from the Indian
Bureau, it seemed desirable that, if possible, we should obtain a

word of approval from the governor of Arizona which we might exhibit as a sort of identification card and certificate of honorable intentions. Accordingly, On July 15th I addressed a letter to Governor Safford, reminding him of my desire to take some of the most influential Apaches on a tour of "the states" in order that they might better comprehend the magnitude of our country, the vastness of our population, and the achievements of our civilization by personal observation and contact, while at the same time many eastern people would have opportunity to acquire a more accurate understanding of the general character of the Apaches, and, as we hoped, a more friendly attitude toward them, and that if the trip was undertaken I hoped to be serving the Indians, the territory, and the general government. I also advised the governor that funds necessary to cover the expense involved had been provided by myself and two friends. Following is the governor's reply:

> Territory of Arizona
> Executive Departent
> Tucson, Arizona
> July 19, 1876.

Mr. John P. Clum,
Tucson, Arizona.

Dear Sir:

    I have received your letter informing me of your contemplated trip through the eastern states with a party of your Apache Indians and asking my opinion as to the propriety of so doing. In reply I have to say that the project appears to me commendable in the highest degree. I know of your efforts to obtain an appropriation from the government for this purpose and much regret you have been unable to obtain such aid.

    I concur heartily in the undertaking and believe it will be conducive of great good. Your Apaches will never appreciate the immensity of our domain, the enterprise and culture of our people, and the advantages of peace until they have mingled with and learned about civilized people by actual contact and practical association.

    Your contemplated trip will therefore be of great benefit to the Indians, and at the same time give the

people of the East a true illustration of the character of
the Apache Indians.

Wishing you success in the undertaking, I am,

> Very sincerely yours,
> A. P. K. Safford,
> Governor.

The next important step was the selection of the personnel of
our party. There were then about 4,500 Indians on the San Carlos
Reservation. We had decided to limit our group of thespians to
twenty, but finally added two boys to this number. This was a
matter of vital importance, demanding the utmost discretion in the
selection of each member with a view to attaining the principal
objectives, namely: the influence to be exerted by the members of
this party after their return to the reservation; the material required
to assure the success of our proposed entertainments; securing a
combination that would maintain harmony among themselves,
while at the same time endeavoring to avoid, as far as possible,
any feeling of disappointment that would embitter any more or
less ambitious candidates who might be left behind. This responsibility devolved entirely upon me because my two associates in
the enterprise were strangers to the Apaches.

The result was that our party of Apache tourists included Es-
kim-in-zin, chief of the Aravaipas, and his wife; Tah-zay, son of
Cochise and chief of the Chiricahuas; Diablo, chief of the
Coyoteros, and his son—five or six years of age; Sagully, chief of
the Yumas [*Yavapais*], and his wife; Casadora, a sub-chief of the
Pinals, and his wife; Captain Jim of the agency Indian police force
and his wife. Ten athletic young braves and a boy about twelve
years of age completed the group. In connection with our
enterprise, the services of Marijildo, that loyal and efficient
interpreter, were indispensable. [*The Chiricahua Apaches kid-
napped Merejildo Grijalva in Sonora when he was about ten. In
1859, at about the age of twenty, he escaped from his captors.
Having become fluent in the Apache language, Grijalva worked as
an interpreter and guide for the American military for many
years.*[1]] Dr. S. B. Chapin, who had been the agency physician,
decided to journey eastward with us. I also employed two
teamsters. With these four men, the twenty-two Indians, and
myself, our party disclosed a grand total of twenty-seven.

The journey from San Carlos to the railroad station at El Moro,
Colorado, was no minor undertaking in itself. The transportation

Merejildo Grijalva (c. 1840-1912), interpreter and guide. Arizona Historical Society, Tucson, #1815.

provided for this part of the trip consisted of one large and substantial farm wagon drawn by four horses, one two-seated light wagon drawn by two horses, and a two-seated covered wagon drawn by four horses, with myself as the Jehu [*driver*] presiding over the reins in the last named conveyance.

Our camp equipment was exceedingly limited—merely a few cooking utensils, a supply of tin cups, tin plates, knives, forks, and spoons, and one or two blankets for each individual. For although the weather was warm, we would attain elevations en route where the nights would be chilly enough. In those days we never thought of carrying tents. Likewise, our commissary supplies were reduced to the lowest terms. Only a few days' rations were carried as we planned to forage on the country through which we were to pass.

The broad mesa upon which the buildings of the San Carlos agency were located presented a gala-day scene on July 29, 1876, the date appointed for our departure upon the long trek in the direction of the rising sun. A great throng of more or less excited Apaches had assembled there to wave and shout a sincere *adieu* and *bon voyage*. Our get-away was most auspicious. We followed up the Gila valley as far as Pueblo Viejo [*near present-day Safford*] and then detoured to the overland stage road, which led us into Silver City, New Mexico. In my files I have found only one newspaper notice regarding our trip through Arizona and New Mexico. This notice was published in the Silver City *Herald* on Saturday, August 5, 1876, from which the following excerpts are quoted:

> John P. Clum, agent at the San Carlos agency, arrived here yesterday with his retinue of Apaches on his way east. This party represents the Aravaipa, Pinal, Coyotero and Chiricahua Apaches. There are sixteen men, four women and two boys. . . . Mr. Clum left San Carlos on Saturday last and it is his intention to make a tour through the East in order to acquaint the Indians with the extent and power of our nation, and to afford them that information which can be obtained only by contact with Eastern enterprise and civilization. He has been careful to select young men of prominence and intelligence who will appreciate the visit and wield a proper influence on their return.
>
> For a year Mr. Clum has endeavored to obtain an appropriation for this purpose but to no effect. He has

now decided to take them at his own expense and will give entertainments in some of the large cities illustrating the true character of these wild Indians both in time of peace and of war. With the proceeds of these exhibitions he hopes to defray all expenses incurred in the tour.

If he meets neither misfortune nor accident we believe this adventure will result in more benefit to the Indians and to the people at large than anything we have yet done for them.

This record shows that we were a full week traveling from the agency to Silver City, and I recall that the entire journey by wagon from San Carlos to El Moro occupied nearly four weeks. From Silver City we drove to the Rio Grande and followed up that valley to old Albuquerque, where we crossed the river and proceeded by the most direct route to old Las Vegas, and from there we followed the old Santa Fe Trail to Trinidad, Colorado, the northernmost outpost of the early Spanish adventurers. At this point we were delighted to learn that we were only four miles from the railway station at El Moro. The fact that it took us nearly a month to drive from the agency to the depot indicates that even as late as 1876 San Carlos was a remote and isolated locality.

However, this somewhat tedious journey to the railroad was not without its compensations. There were many far-flung and inspiring scenic vistas as we passed valley and mesa and mountain in that semi-arid region of the Southwest. There was an invigorating tonic in the fresh, clean, rare atmosphere, and the wide, open spaces impressed a sense of boundless freedom, at the same time inviting a more intimate communion with Nature that was both exhilarating and uplifting. Also, happily, we had robust health and the vigor of youth which enabled us to appreciate and enjoy these picturesque and romantic features to the utmost and to minimize the less agreeable experiences.

Our plan to forage on the country as we traveled proved most satisfactory. At convenient intervals I purchased a small steer or a couple of sheep which were speedily killed and dressed by the Indians. Other supplies were obtained from the merchants in the towns through which we passed.

For the most part the Indians enjoyed the trip and maintained their normal spirit of good humor, so that when we arrived at El Moro all the members of our expedition were still on cordial speaking terms, which is not always true of more civilized parties

at the end of a journey of this character. We had at least one very
uncomfortable experience en route. A rain of cloudburst
proportions overtook us one afternoon in the Rio Grande valley
and continued for several hours. We were drenched. Cooking was
impossible. Our supper consisted of cold beans—straight—and
we passed the night in an exceedingly damp and disagreeable
fashion.

It will be proper to record here our solitary clash with the
minions of the law en route. This occurred at old Albuquerque.
We camped for the night in the suburbs of that venerable city and,
while our herders slept, our horses invaded an adjacent corn field
and munched and trampled some of the growing corn. The next
morning I was haled before the austere Alcalde [*magistrate*], who
evinced an unfriendly spirit as soon as he learned that we were
Apaches from the wilds of Arizona, and without hesitation he
assessed the damages to the corn at *veinte pesos* [*twenty dollars*]
and demanded immediate payment thereof. When I protested that
the amount seemed excessive his honor flung at me his fiercest
war-like glare, pounded upon a volume of the statutes and shouted
from the bench, *"La ley es la ley!"* [*The law is the law!*], at the
same time threatening to summon the entire population of the city,
if necessary, to enforce the judgement of the honorable court. This
bit of comedy appealed so keenly to my sense of humor that I
prolonged and accentuated the horse-play a bit by designedly
contributing to the irritation of the high and mighty Alcalde,
although I had no desire to avoid payment for the damage our
horses had done to the innocent Mexican's corn. Finally the
twenty good American dollars were delivered into the custody of
the court, the cantankerous Alcalde was pacified, and we Apaches
were permitted to go on our way rejoicing.

Another wayside incident may prove of interest as illustrating
the fact that the Apaches in our party had no conception of the
vast area of the United States or of the millions of the paleface
race then occupying those sections of our country we were about
to visit. In a general way the frontiersmen and the pioneer settlers
knew something of the tragic fate of all the Indian tribes that had
opposed the white men in their resistless advance from Plymouth
Rock to the Rocky Mountains, and, judging the future by the past,
they were confident that sooner or later the Apaches must yield to
their prowess—hence they were impatient at the persistent
resistance offered by these redskins of the mountains.

But the Apaches had no hint of the sad tragedies which,
through the passing decades, had overtaken tribe after tribe of the

aborigines who had formerly held sway over that vast territory stretching from the big sea on the east to the big mountains on the west. To the Apaches the white men were always intruders, and, as a rule, aggressors. Because at first these intruders had appeared in small numbers the Apaches doubted the boasted "man-power" of the paleface, and, therefore, they felt equal to the task of opposing and even of destroying those adventurous pioneers who came from time to time to spy out their country and to appropriate whatever pleased them for the time being, or promised advantage or profit for the future.

In a general way the personal observations of the Apaches had been confined to southeastern Arizona, southwestern New Mexico and northern Chihuahua and Sonora, where there were comparatively few white settlers. On this trip we had passed through the eastern half of Arizona and across the entire Territory of New Mexico and had observed that the country was still undeveloped and but sparsely settled. We had been traveling northeastward nearly a month and were now approaching the Colorado line without having seen any substantial evidences of the alleged progress and prowess of the white race.

This situation furnished the framework for the wayside incident referred to. The day's journey had not been tiresome, the evening meal had been disposed of with keen relish, and now the Indians were gathered about their community camp fire, smoking cigarettes and relating experiences of a more or less thrilling nature. I had already spread my blankets on the ground and was lying there contemplating the glories of that August night, the drive we were about to make over the Raton range, and our near approach to the railroad. I was abruptly recalled from these very pleasing ruminations when Marijildo came over from the circle of Indians and with evident concern, told me that Tah-zay "was not talking right." Tah-zay was the elder son of Cochise, the famous head chief of the Chiricahuas who had been a terror to all who had ventured to intrude within the range of his territory until a treaty of peace was arranged between him and General Howard in the fall of 1872. Cochise died in 1874 and Tah-zay succeeded his father as head chief of the Chiricahuas. And now Marijildo told me this young chief had been boasting to his traveling companions of the wonderful prowess of his people; that he had been relating in detail several deadly battles which had occurred prior to the treaty made with General Howard, in each of which the Chiricahuas had triumphed valiantly over their paleface foes; and that Tah-zay had concluded his vivid and spirited recital by declaring with evident pride and confidence that it was a good thing the treaty had been made with his father four years before, otherwise there would have been very few white people left alive at the time he was speaking.

"Don't be alarmed," I said to Marijildo. "Let Tah-zay enjoy his dream a little longer if it pleases him. In a couple of days we will be on the railroad, and then very soon we will see something of homes and farms and villages and cities of the white man's country. Doubtless these exhibits will prove a revelation to the boastful young chief."

At El Moro we reached what the Apaches called the "pesh-be-tin"—the road of iron. It was but natural that the Indians should manifest genuine interest in the railroad—and particularly in the locomotives—and yet there was no undue excitement when we boarded the train. However, soon after the train started a couple of the women began crying. When I asked the reason they said they feared they would never see San Carlos again. As long as we were traveling with the wagons amid the mesas and the mountains they remained unconcerned, but now that we were on a railway train bound for Washington—with the mountains behind us and the vast plains ahead of us—they were alarmed. But they very soon recovered their accustomed equanimity, and the entire party made the trip to Philadelphia and return like veteran tourists.

I endeavored to observe carefully the effect of the first contact with civilization upon the several members of our party as we passed through Pueblo and Denver and Kansas City and climbed to the summit of the dome of the city hall at Saint Louis and were finally quartered in Cincinnati. Then, as we stood in a balcony on the second story of our hotel and looked down upon the congested traffic in the street below, I asked the Indians what they thought of the country and the villages of the paleface race. Es-kim-in-zin protested that he was unable to express his feelings, and, waving his hand about his head, he said that all the very wonderful sights made him "dizzy."

Tah-zay was silent. He did not know what Marijildo had told me concerning his wayside boasting, and so I could ask him in an innocent was if he did not think his father had acted wisely in making peace with the white men. The young Chiricahua chief was still proud of his people, but he admitted that he now realized how unequal their fight had been. The anticipated benefits of this trip were already apparent. I was much gratified, little dreaming that the stalwart and genial Tah-zay would never return to the country and the people he loved so well.

If the Indians were immensely interested in what they saw in the populous and busy camps of the white men, it must also be recorded that the palefaces were quite as much interested in the presence of this company of "wild" Apaches fresh from the remote waste places of Arizona. And this interest was keenly accentuated by thoughts of the recent fatal conflict between General Custer's command and the Sioux, for be it remembered that if there was any tribe of Indians in the country at that time whose reputation as desperate and deadly warriors exceeded that of the Sioux, it was the Apaches of Arizona.

And thus it happened that whenever we appeared upon the streets of the large cities we were speedily surrounded by a milling throng of curious people, each one eager to obtain an intimate view of these Indians. Although the extermination of Custer and his brave comrades had aroused a popular sentiment against the Indians in general, I am glad to be able to testify that no demonstration of a hostile character occurred during our visit to the several states, notwithstanding the fact that the active services of the police were frequently necessary to enable us to pass through the crowds that blocked our progress in the streets of the big cities.

While we were traveling with the wagons and camping in the open air the Indians cooked and ate as they had always been accustomed to do in and about their native wiki-ups, but as soon as we were embarked on the railroad and entered the cities of the middle West the necessity for a complete readjustment of our "table manners" was imperative, and this readjustment was thrust upon us with heartless abruptness. But the Apaches demonstrated their ability to rise to the occasion, and very soon they were able to sit comfortably at the table, eat their food from plates, and handle their knives and forks with reasonable ease and commendable accuracy. Another tribute I desire to record in favor of these representatives of the untutored redskins of the mountains of the Southwest is the fact that no complaint alleging rude and boisterous conduct or uncleanliness on their part was made to me by those conducting the hotels and boarding houses where the Apaches were quartered in the several cities visited by us.

Finally the fateful period had arrived when the histrionic talents of our aboriginal actors and the financial outcome of our enterprise were to be put to the acid test in the initial entertainment to be given by the Indians. If I had not realized before the daring character of this undertaking, I did so to the last degree when I began to arrange the plot and to assign the characters and to instruct the individual Indians in the roles they were to enact in this drama of the Arizona frontier. The plan and purpose to rehearse this raw material in the exacting details of the several "tableaux" with such satisfactory results as would enable us to present the entire spectacle in a manner to attract and captivate an audience of blase theatre fans and thus transform these "wild" Apaches into star actors in a single week, was, indeed, such a bold ambition as only the most optimistic might hope to accomplish. But the overcoming of seemingly insurmountable obstacles had been an inspiring feature of my job ever since I assumed the direction of the affairs of the Apaches, and so our rehearsals proceeded merrily with no thought of failure. It should be stated, however, that the most difficult and serious feature of the play was made possible by the fact that Dr. Chapin, Marijildo (who was a Mexican), and myself represented the paleface foes of the Indians in the desperate mock fighting on the stage and the Apaches knew that we would play the game on the square.

Our confidence in the intelligence, ability, and loyal cooperation of our Apache actors was indicated by the fact that the date of our first appearance was announced when we were just beginning the rehearsals. Fortunately, the stage manager developed a sincere and sympathetic interest in our unique Wild West play and our "savage" players. He very soon appreciated that, although we were all "raw recruits," we were exceedingly anxious to present a really good show, and he gave us most valuable suggestions and assistance, for which I thanked him then—and thank him now.

We made our debut at Saint Louis, Missouri, and emerged from our premier performance without a single fatality or even inciting an incipient riot. Fortunately, I have preserved two exhibits of the literature announcing the birth of our stage career—a program and a press notice. I am, therefore, able to include in this narrative a facsimile of the program and a copy of the press notice. The program will serve to indicate the somewhat ambitious character of our entertainment. The following is a copy of the press notice which was published in a Saint Louis morning paper on Saturday, September 9, 1876:

OLYMPIC THEATRE

Considering the popular feeling against the noble red man at present, the entertainment given at the Olympic

Theatre last night by the tribe of Apache Indians of Arizona under the supervision of ex-Agent John P. Clum was well patronized. The dress circle contained many ladies, the upper tier was crowded with the gamins [*street urchins*] of the city, and in the parquette were to be seen four Celestials [*Chinese*], who sat near the stage and seemed to enjoy the performance as much as anybody. These Indians had only been in the city about a week and knew little or nothing of what a great city was or even what a theatre was like until their arrival. They have only had a few rehearsals, but even these have not fully convinced them that it is altogether proper and right that they should publicly exhibit their manners and customs or dance their war-dance behind the footlights. For a first effort they did very well last night, however, many of their tableaux being strikingly realistic as well as picturesque.

The troupe numbers sixteen braves and four squaws, and when the curtain went up they appeared before the audience in full costumes. That is to say, they were naked from the waist up, but their chests, backs, arms, necks and faces were painted with all the colors of the rainbow. Mr. Clum introduced them in a brief speech, after which they retired to prepare for the second tableau. This represented an Indian encampment where the braves are surprised as they sing their peculiar and monotonous song around their campfire. A hand-to-hand combat ensues, resulting in the triumph of the palefaces. There was considerable fighting done, however, and when the knife of the white man gleamed in the face of the Indian, who was held in his strong embrace, the applause, especially from the galleries, was deafening.

The third tableau was an Indian council of war, with speeches by the braves and chiefs. Of course the audience applauded each speech at the right point. The most ludicrous tableau of the whole performance, however, was that representing an Indian woman mourning the death of her husband. What was meant to be pathetic, and what is without doubt affecting when done at the proper time and place, was really the funniest part of the show. An Indian woman comes out with an old blanket thrown over her head and shoulders, and kneeling on the ground shakes her head and utters the most dismal cries. To an American audience her voice conveys not the slightest emotion of grief, and when she boo-hoos they can only see a performance that causes their sides to shake with laughter. The fifth tableau disclosed the braves in a grand war-dance, which was one of the best things done during the evening.

Part second changed the program by allowing the red man a victory over the paleface, the former making the attack. Included in this was the Indian scalp-dance. The final tableau showed the Indians at home, engaged in social games and as happy and contented as any white man. The entire performance was enjoyable. There will be a matinee at two o'clock today and another performance in the evening, the last to be given in this city.

It is to be regretted that the scalping acts were included in our program, for I now firmly believe that this was wholly unwarranted so far as the Apaches were concerned. A popular notion then prevailed—and still survives—assuming that in every successful combat between warriors of the redskin and paleface races, the victor invariably crowned his conquest by lifting the scalp of his fallen foe. While it is alleged that the exquisitely cruel act of scalping an enemy was a common practice among the Indians who roamed over the vast plains, as well as among some of the eastern tribes, I am now satisfied that the Apaches did not scalp their victims, at least I have never been confronted with competent evidence establishing a single act of this character. The very friendly and efficient stage manager at Saint Louis advised that our combat scenes should include the taking of the scalp in order to conform to the popular idea of the details of such deadly affairs. In the midst of our hectic preparations for the show the suggestion of the stage manager was adopted without due consideration. It was a serious mistake, and the only feature of our program not sustained by the facts. The research involved in the preparation of this story has brought the offending feature of our exhibition to my attention, and I make haste to set the record of the Apaches right in this particular.

We gave a good show—*we* even admitted that. In at least two tableaux we presented the "real stuff" with a dash of action and excitement that was enough to thrill even a hard-boiled frontiersman. At each entertainment we shot and cut and killed each other (in realistic stage fashion). *We delivered the goods.* But notwithstanding favorable comments from individuals and the press our theatrical venture did not prove a financial success. In such circumstances "post mortems" yield little satisfaction. However, it is doubtless true that we were the innocent victims of the unfriendly sentiment occasioned by the killing of Custer and his command. Furthermore, we may have overestimated the public confidence in our thoroughbred, untutored, and unrestrained actors of the redskin race. During the scenes in which mock fighting occurred these "wild" Apaches, hideous in their war-paint, dashed and leaped about the stage firing rifles, flashing Bowie knives, and causing the painted forests and canyons of the scenery to echo with their savage, blood-curdling war-whoops. Nothing but the footlights separated them from the audience, and it is not improbable that there were many who would have been glad to witness the spectacle if they had been confident that the Indians, wrought up to a high pitch of excitement by the realistic play, would not break from our control, go "wild" and see "red," and extend their raid across the footlights into the audience.

Whatever may have been the reason, we were persistently confronted with the disagreeable fact that each successive entertainment left us with less available cash on hand. And thus it happened that we quit the show business, packed up our fancy buckskin suits, beaded moccasins, Bowie knives, etc., and proceeded to Washington to view the national capital and to interview the Great White Father. While there we explored the Capitol building and the White House, voyaged down the Potomac to Mount Vernon, and detoured for a picnic in the mountains of Virginia. Of course, we had several conferences with the Commissioner of Indian Affairs.

However, our visit to Washington was sadly marred by the only tragedy of the trip—the death of the young Chiricahua chief, Tah-zay. Young and strong as he was, Tah-zay fell ill with pneumonia, and although the best medical skill available was called to attend him he grew worse rapidly and died within a few days. The funeral services were conducted by Rev. J. E. Rankin of the First Congregational Church of Washington. Among those attending the obsequies were Commissioner of Indian Affairs J. Q. [*John Quincy*] Smith and General O. O. Howard, who, four years previous, had made the treaty of peace with Cochise, the dead Apache's father. The interment was made in the Congressional Cemetery. The illness and death of Tah-zay were

not devoid of beneficial results for the reason that they afforded
the Indians with our party an opportunity to observe the civilized
methods and customs of caring for the sick and preparing the dead
for burial, as well as our funeral rites and ceremonies, all of
which, under ordinary circumstances, were about the last things I
would have thought of bringing to their particular attention. [*The
Chiricahuas at San Carlos saw no bright side to Taza's death.
When they learned of his demise they immediately assumed that
the Whites had poisoned him or killed him with witchcraft. Clum
was hard pressed to convince them otherwise, and things could
have gotten ugly if Eskiminzin had not interceded on his behalf.*[2]]

*Taza, eldest son of
Cochise. Arizona
Historical Society,
Tucson, #894.*

When we stopped at Saint Louis I learned that Commissioner
Smith was then in that city opening bids for certain Indian
supplies. The coming of the Apaches had been widely broadcast
by the press, and when I called upon the commissioner at his hotel
I anticipated a proper official "panning" for having absented
myself and the Indians from the reservation without permission
from the Indian Bureau. But, on the contrary, Commissioner
Smith greeted me cordially, inquired how the Apaches were
enjoying their trip, and then, quite abruptly but with earnestness,
he said: "Mr. Clum, you are going back to San Carlos."

I told the commissioner frankly why I had resigned and that I had not expected to return to San Carlos as agent, that I was still hopeful that the entertainments we expected to give would prove satisfactory and beneficial to all concerned, and therefore my thoughts and plans were centered upon this enterprise. Commissioner Smith extended his best wishes for our success, but I suspected that he was reserving the right to doubt that our anticipations would be realized from a financial viewpoint. It was not so long after this interview until the very unsatisfactory returns from the box-offices had convinced me that the commissioner's doubts had been well founded.

Some of the San Carlos thespians in Washington, D.C. Front row: Chiquito, Eskiminzin, Sagully, Casadora. Middle row: wife of Chiquito, wife of Eskiminzin, wife of Casadora. Back row: Merejildo Grijalva, John Clum. Smithsonian Institution, Washington, D.C., #NAA 31,374-B.

Soon after our arrival in Washington I called upon Commissioner Smith at his office in the Interior Department and advised him of the sad fate of our brief and hectic "stage career." His attitude was sympathetic, and he said that while he regretted the enterprise had resulted in financial loss to my two friends and myself, he hoped the experience had left me in a mood to withdraw my resignation and resume my duties as agent at San Carlos. During the period of Tah-zay's illness we had ample time to discuss all the dips, spurs, and angles of the general situation in Arizona. Finally, the commissioner proposed that if I would withdraw my resignation and resume charge of the 4,500 Apaches then on the San Carlos Reservation that the Interior Department would petition Congress for an increase in my salary; that I would not be asked to undertake any more "foreign" expeditions for the purpose of removing other tribes to my reservation; that certain specified necessary agency equipment would be purchased; that in the execution of my official duties I would be given the fullest support by the officials of the Indian Bureau; and that because of the obvious benefits of the trip to the Apaches accompanying me, their visit would be approved and their expenses returning to the reservation would be paid by the Interior Department. Encouraged by these stipulations I withdrew my resignation and set about arranging for the return trip to San Carlos.

The following official communications are of interest in connection with the resignation submitted by me on February 27, 1876, which made it possible for me to invade the East with the Apache thespians:

(TELEGRAM)

Washington, D.C.
March 20, 1876.

Agent Clum,
San Carlos, Arizona.

Secretary Interior has accepted your resignation to take effect upon appointment of successor.

J. Q. Smith, Commissioner,
Office of Indian Affairs.

(LETTER)

Washington, D.C.
October 25, 1876.

Mr. John P. Clum,
U.S. Indian Agent,
Washington, D.C.

Sir: . . . and in view of the further fact that upon the request of this office you have withdrawn your resignation, you will be allowed your actual and necessary traveling expenses in returning.

Yours respectfully,
S. A. Galpin, Acting Commissioner,
Office of Indian Affairs.

Conspicuous mention should be made of the persistent good humor and harmony that prevailed among this little company of Apaches throughout the trip. It should be remembered that our party was composed of representatives of distinct bands of a nomadic race, which, until quite recently, had occupied widely separated hunting and camping grounds, and, therefore, the Coyoteros and the Aravaipas and the Chiricahuas had not had opportunity to establish intimate acquaintances and lifelong friendships. In fact, several of the more prominent members of the party were just getting acquainted with each other on this trip, and yet in all the vicissitudes of that remarkable visit to the East there was no wrangling among the members of our group. And, looking backward, I have always regarded it as most remarkable that we were able to make that long, tedious trek by team to take those Indians so far from their homeland to meet conditions new and strange to them without developing a single instance which would indicate that any members of the group were inharmonious, hostile, or antagonistic among themselves.

We experience only one vicious outburst of hostility toward the Apaches en route, and this, I am pleased to say, expressed the attitude of only one man. The incident occurred while we were homeward bound. One evening as we were passing through a Middle Western state, a robust, black whiskered, and grim visaged conductor entered the car in which the Indians were traveling. I chanced to be in the car at the time and was conversing with two or three other passengers near the door through which the conductor entered. He glanced savagely at the Indians and exclaimed: "The ------ ---- -- -------, I'd like to have every scalp hanging to my belt." "Why so?" I ventured to inquire, "have these Indians harmed you or your family or your friends?" "No," he snapped back, "they have not, but they are a bunch of blood-thirsty savages—the damned red devils," etc. After he had emitted a little more similar rough stuff I pointed to Es-kim-in-zin and mentioned some of the wrongs he had suffered at the hands of the white race: the cruel massacre of his family and friends [*near Camp Grant in 1871*], his imprisonment at hard labor in chains, etc., and then I added, "That man is an Indian—an Apache. You call him a 'blood-thirsty savage,' and yet he says he has no desire for revenge, that he wants to forget past wrongs and live a good and useful life. That's the kind of savage he is, and yet he has always lived in the Arizona mountains, while you have enjoyed the advantages of Christian civilization. What do you mean by 'blood-thirsty?' What kind of a savage are you?" The menacing glance he flashed at me bespoke the hot blood of cruel barbarian forebears that surged in his veins. "Who has the tickets?" he snarled. I handed him the tickets and the incident was closed.

It was deemed worth while that the return trip should be made by way of Philadelphia in order that the Indians might have a glimpse of the Centennial Exposition. This was done, and then we proceeded direct to El Moro, Colorado, where the teams and teamsters were in readiness for the journey overland to San Carlos. And the morning after our arrival at El Moro the little caravan moved westward in the charge of Marijildo and two other agency employees, while I returned once more to the East for the purpose of acquiring a young bride, who had consented to share with me the vicissitudes of life on an Arizona Indian reservation with 4,500 other "wild" Apaches.

NOTES AND CITATIONS

Chapter 1. Newspapers and Stage Robbers

1. Lutrell 1949.
2. Brown, Rollin C., unpublished ms.
3. Lutrell 1949.
4. Carmony 1994, pp. 193-194.
5. Lutrell 1949.
6. Myrick 1975, pp. 51, 54, 61.
7. Lutrell 1949.
8. John P. Clum Collection, Special Collections Department, University of Arizona Library; Ryan 1965a. Clayton (1985) discovered that Woodworth Clum's full name was Henry Woodworth Clum. However, Woodworth never used the name Henry, nor did family members mention the name in their writings.
9. Byrkit 1980.

Chapter 2. The Trek to Tombstone

1. Lutrell 1949; Ryan 1965a; *Arizona Quarterly Illustrated*, October 1880, January 1881; *Tombstone (Weekly) Epitaph*, April 11, 1881.
2. Lutrell 1949.
3. Theobald and Theobald 1961.
4. Theobald and Theobald 1961. *Tombstone Epitaph*, June 12, 1880. On June 22, 1880, George M. Perine and Buckskin Frank Leslie got in a row with Mike Killeen, and Killeen was killed. Both Leslie and Perine were arrested for murder, but neither man was convicted in the affair (Martin 1951, pp. 82-91; Bailey 1996, pp. 57, 76, 78).
5. Underhill 1979; Traywick 1988.
6. Chaput 1994a, pp. 57-60.
7. Miller and Snell 1963; DeArment 1979; Turner 1980, p. 17.
8. Ball 1978, pp. 117, 123; Erwin 1993, p. 164; Chaput 1994a, pp. 52, 59.
9. Bailey 1996, pp. 128-129.
10. Traywick 1994e, pp. 132, 133. Some writers have stated or implied that Wyatt resigned as deputy Pima County sheriff *before* the November 1880 general election. Actually, Wyatt resigned on November 9, a week *after* the election, which was

held on November 2 (Bailey 1996, p. 100).

11. *Tombstone Epitaph*, November 12, 1880, "Sheriff Shibell has appointed John Behan as deputy sheriff for Tombstone."

12. Acts of Arizona's Eleventh Territorial Legislature, 1881.

13. Turner 1981, pp. 142-143, 166. Virtually every writer who has addressed the subject has stated that Wyatt Earp was a Republican. Indeed, in the 1870s Wyatt dabbled in Republican politics in Kansas, a predominantly Republican state (*Dodge City Times*, August 17, 1878). Moreover, late in life Wyatt told a newspaper reporter that he usually supported Republican candidates for president (Bell 1995, p. 123). But his political posture in Arizona may have been different. An article published in the May 27, 1882, San Francisco *Examiner* quoted Virgil Earp as saying, "I am a Republican. My brothers are Democrats." (Virgil was in San Francisco seeking medical help for an injured arm.) If Virgil's remarks were accurately reported and Wyatt had declared himself a Democrat upon arriving in Arizona, it would help explain why Pima County Sheriff Charles Shibell, a Democrat, hired Wyatt as his deputy. It would also clarify why Governor Frémont, a Republican, appointed a Democrat (John Behan) to be Cochise County's first sheriff. If the leading candidates for the job, Behan and Earp, were both Democrats, the governor would have had no real alternative. Also, it would seem a bit unusual for Democrat Behan to offer to hire Wyatt as his undersheriff if Wyatt was a staunch Republican. The man Behan finally appointed to the position, Harry Woods, was a Democrat. Lastly, the Earp family appears to have had Democratic roots. The father of the brothers, Nicholas P. Earp, ran for public office in California as a Democrat (*San Diego Union*, August 16, 1884, August 21, 1884). No document from the early 1880s in which Wyatt Earp stated his party affiliation has come to my attention. The *Examiner* article is reprinted in Chaput 1994a, pages 235-242.

14. Marks 1989, pp. 170-176; Traywick 1996a, pp. 59-81; Gatto 1995, pp. 117-127; Johnson 1996, pp. 153-166.

15. Martin 1951, pp. 58-61; *Tombstone Epitaph*, April 19, 1881 (reprinted in Traywick 1994d, p. 44). Most authorities agree that Johnny-behind-the-deuce's name was John O'Rourke, yet others maintain that Michael O'Rourke is correct. The authentic names of frontier drifters such as Johnny, men who often used nicknames and aliases, are difficult to determine with certainty.

16. Walker 1979; Marks 1989, pp. 56-57, 112-113, 115-116.
17. Ryan 1966; Clayton 1985; *Tombstone Epitaph*, June 9, 1881.
18. Ryan 1966.
19. Bailey 1997; Ryan 1966; *Tombstone Epitaph*, April 10, 1885.
20. Bailey 1996, p. 207.
21. Bailey 1997.
22. C. W. Clum family records, Montgomery County Historical Society Library, Rockville, Maryland; Gimbert 1988.
23. *Tombstone Daily Nugget*, May 11, 1882; Ryan 1966; Bailey 1996, p. 227.
24. Bailey 1996, p. 64. In 1879 the Tombstone townsite was surveyed and streets, blocks, and lots delineated on maps. On June 23, 1880, Clum paid $1,000 for a 99-year lease on lots 5 and 6 in block 35 to Edward Field and Horatio S. Sanford, the owners of the Gilded Age Mining Claim. On April 22, 1882, Clum paid $300 to Tombstone Townsite Company officials James S. Clark, John D. Rouse, and John J. Anderson for a quit-claim deed renouncing their interest in the same two lots. Photocopies of these documents are in the John P. Clum Collection, Special Collections Department, University of Arizona Library. See Walker 1979 for a discussion of the ownership of Tombstone town lots controversy.
25. Bailey 1996, p. 111-112; *Tombstone Epitaph*, December 19, 1880.
26. Bailey 1996, p. 141.
27. Parker, Marjorie Clum, unpublished ms. in the Wallace Clayton Collection, Arizona Historical Society, Tucson.
28. *Tombstone Daily Nugget*, July 9, 1881.
29. Parker 1972; Clayton 1985.
30. See Bailey 1996, pp. 114-117, for George Parsons' remarks about his role in electing Clum mayor of Tombstone. Parsons later became upset when Clum and the council failed to appoint him city auditor. He thought the position had been promised to him, but Seward B. Chapin got the job instead (Bailey 1996, pp. 134, 138).
31. "The City Election," *Tombstone Epitaph*, January 5, 1881. The editor could not locate a complete copy of this issue of the *Epitaph*. A collector of Tombstone documents kindly provided the editor with a photocopy of this article, which gives the results of the January 4, 1881, Tombstone municipal election.
32. Acts of Arizona's Eleventh Territorial Legislature, 1881.
33. Walker 1979; Erwin 1993, p. 149; *Arizona Weekly Citizen*, December 13, 1879, "Tombstone Notes."

34. *Arizona Weekly Star*, January 8, 1880.
35. Bailey 1996, p. 134.
36. Marks (1989, pp. 135-154) gives a coherent discussion of the confusing aftermath of the March 1881 attack on the Benson stage. See also Erwin 1993, pp. 237-250; Gatto 1995, pp. 101-112; Traywick 1996b, pp. 97-102; and Johnson 1996, pp. 134-138.
37. Walker 1979; Erwin 1993, p. 149.
38. *Arizona Weekly Star*, January 8, 1880.
39. Martin 1951, pp. 177-178.
40. Tombstone Common Council minutes.
41. Bailey 1996, p. 99.
42. Erwin 1993, pp. 173-174, 177.
43. Tombstone Common Council minutes.
44. The source of this erroneous scenario may be Waters 1960 (p. 118). But regardless of its origin, placing Virgil Earp in the January 1881 election as Sippy's challenger has caused confusion. Both Clum and Sippy ran in this contest on the Citizens' Protective Party ticket—they were on the same political team (*Tombstone Epitaph*, January 4, 1881). If Earp was on the ballot he would have been running against the candidate and party supported by Clum. But weren't Earp and Clum generally allies? How did they come to be on opposite sides in this case? The answer to the puzzle is that Virgil Earp didn't run for marshal of Tombstone in January 1881.
45. *Tombstone Epitaph*, January 5, 1881. Clum (1929b) and Lake (1931, p. 246) correctly identified Sippy's opponent in the January 1881 election as Howard Lee.
46. Bailey 1996, p. 141.
47. Martin 1951, pp. 125-128; Bailey 1996, pp. 155-158, 235-245.
48. *Tombstone Epitaph*, April 17, 1881, "An ordinance to provide for a police department of the City of Tombstone . . . ."
49. Tombstone Common Council minutes; Marks 1989, pp. 155-156; Chaput 1994a, p. 92.
50. Martin 1951, pp. 182-183; Johnson 1996, pp. 167-168. Some Tombstone documents refer to Pete "Spencer," others to Pete "Spence." Which spelling is correct is hard to ascertain.

Chapter 3. Geronimo Breaks Loose

1. Collins 1994, p. 32.
2. Collins 1994, p. 32.
3. Debo 1976.

4. Collins 1994, pp. 24-27.
5. Edwin Sweeney, personal communication.
6. Bailey 1996, p. 180. George Parsons described the expedition to intercept Geronimo. See Bailey 1996, pp. 180-184.
7. Debo 1976.

Chapter 4. The Earp-Clanton Battle

1. Martin 1951, pp. 246-247. Some modern writers spell the lynched man's name "Heith" (for example Ball 1992 and Chaput 1995).
2. Ball 1992, p. 382.
3. Tombstone Common Council minutes, April 19, 1881; *Tombstone Epitaph*, April 27, 1881, "An ordinance to provide against the carrying of deadly weapons."
4. Turner 1981, pp. 162, 172, 192.
5. Turner 1981, p. 190.
6. Ball 1992, pp. 29-30.
7. Erwin 1993, p. 268.
8. Turner 1981, pp. 217-226.
9. Tombstone Common Council minutes; Chaput 1994a, pp. 137, 144, 151; Traywick 1994d, p. 174.
10. Clum 1929b; Martin 1951, p. 158.
11. Rosa 1993, pp. 182-183.
12. Chaput 1995.
13. Chaput 1995, pp. 65-70.
14. Martin 1951, pp. 236-249.
15. Martin 1951, p. 242; Traywick 1994e, p. 171.
16. Chaput 1995.

Chapter 5. Adieu to the Earps

1. Martin 1951, pp. 155-156.
2. Bell 1995, p. 119; Sonnichsen 1982, p. 108.
3. See Martin 1951, pp. 155-158, Clum 1929b (appendix), and Traywick 1994d, pp. 35-36 for the *Epitaph's* articles regarding this incident.
4. *Tombstone Epitaph*, January 4, 1882.
5. Theobald and Theobald 1961.
6. Ball 1978, p. 123; Chaput 1994a, pp. 150-151.
7. *Tombstone Epitaph*, February 3, 1882, "The Clanton Trial." Marks 1989, pp. 332-333.
8. Martin 1951, pp. 221-223; *Tombstone Epitaph*, March 22,

1882, "The Coroner's Verdict;" *Tombstone Epitaph*, March 23, 1882, "Coroner's Inquest on the Body of the Late Morgan S. Earp."

9. Martin 1951, p. 217-218; Myrick 1975, p. 274; *Tombstone Epitaph*, January 13, 1882, "The First Passenger Train to Contention . . . . The regular trains will commence running on the 1st of February."

10. Carmony 1994, p. 228.

11. Martin 1951, p. 219.

12. Martin 1951, p. 225; Marks 1989, p. 366.

13. *Tombstone Epitaph*, March 23, 1882, "Search for the Earp Party;" Breakenridge 1928, p. 298; Marks 1989, p. 351; Gatto 1995, p. 163.

14. Martin 1951, p. 225.

15. Marks 1989, pp. 351-354; Johnson 1996, pp. 189-190, 203.

16. Martin 1951, pp. 226-234; *Tombstone Daily Nugget*, April 1, 1882, "Come, Now . . . . The NUGGET has said Curly William is alive." Breakenridge 1928, pp. 291-297; Marks 1989, pp. 356-360; Gatto 1995, pp. 165-169; Johnson 1996, pp. 190-191.

17. Ball 1978, p. 125; Ball 1992, p. 219. Exactly when Wyatt and Virgil gave up their deputy U.S. marshal badges isn't clear. The February 2, 1882, *Epitaph* published an article titled "The Deputy Marshalship" in which it was reported that a citizens' committee recommended John H. Jackson and Silas Bryant to U.S. Marshal Crawley Dake (who was visiting Tombstone) for deputy marshal appointments to replace the embattled and controversial Earps. Dake agreed to appoint one of the recommended men "in proper time." The same issue of the *Epitaph* published a letter of resignation as deputy marshals signed by Virgil and Wyatt Earp. The letter was dated February 1 and was addressed to Marshal Dake (the letter is reprinted in Traywick 1994d, p. 174). However, it appears that Dake did not act on their resignations immediately. Articles in the February 28, 1882, *Nugget* indicate that Dake had appointed John Jackson a deputy but had not yet removed the Earps from his roster of subordinates. Virgil Earp left the territory in late March 1882 and his resignation must have been finalized about that time. Erwin (1993, pp. 387-389) reproduced an 1885 document stating that Wyatt Earp sent another letter of resignation to Dake after fleeing Arizona in April 1882.

18. Lutrell 1949.

19. *Tombstone Epitaph*, January 4, 1882.

Chapter 6. Booms and Depressions

1. *Tombstone Epitaph*, June 2, 1882.
2. Martin 1951, pp. 268-287; Traywick 1994a, pp. 11-20; Bailey 1997.
3. *Dictionary of American Biography.*
4. Theobald and Theobald 1961.
5. Bailey 1997, p. 194. Parsons' is the only reference to "Caroline" Clum the editor has found. In later years she and her family seem to have used the name "Caro" exclusively. "Caro" is undoubtedly short for "Caroline," but the word means "beloved" in Spanish and this may have been a factor in the family's preference for it.
6. Theobald and Theobald 1961; Tombstone Common Council minutes.
7. *Tombstone Epitaph*, February 19, 1886. Ryan 1966; Bailey 1997 (George Parsons acted in this production).
8. Mrs. McNeil was Bessie McNeil, the wife of Donald Alston McNeil, a Tombstone businessman. Records show that Bessie (Elizabeth?) Brown married Donald A. McNeil in Tombstone in 1884. Christine Rhodes, Cochise County Recorder, Bisbee, Arizona, personal communication. Larry McFall, Tombstone Courthouse State Historical Park, personal communication.
9. Tombstone Common Council minutes.

Chapter 7. The Capture of Geronimo

1. Bernard Fontana, personal communication.
2. Sweeney 1992.
3. Carmony 1994, p. 103.
4. Debo 1976.
5. Ball 1992.
6. Thrapp 1974.
7. Debo 1976.
8. Carmony 1994, p. 125, 158.

Chapter 8. Apaches as Thespians

1. Sweeney 1992.
2. Clum 1928b; Clum 1936, p. 199-201; Ball 1970, pp. 51-52.

SOURCES AND REFERENCES

Altshuler, Constance Wynn. 1983. *Starting With Defiance: Nineteenth Century Arizona Military Posts.* Arizona Historical Society, Tucson.

_____. 1991. *Cavalry Yellow & Infantry Blue: Army Officers in Arizona Between 1851 and 1886.* Arizona Historical Society, Tucson.

Anon. 1880. "Tombstone Election." *Arizona Weekly Star* (Tucson), January 8. (On January 6, 1880, Alder Randall was elected mayor of Tombstone, defeating B. A. Fickas; Fred White defeated D. S. Miller in the contest for town marshal.)

_____. 1880. "California dispatches announce the appointment of John P. Clum to be Postmaster at Tombstone." *Tombstone Epitaph*, June 12.

_____. 1880. "Col. John P. Clum." *Arizona Quarterly Illustrated*, Vol. I, No. 2 (October), p. 12.

_____. 1880. "In memoriam. Another heart is stifled in eternal silence . . . ." *Tombstone Epitaph*, December 19. (Notice of Mary Clum's death. Photocopy of article in editor's files.)

_____. 1881. "Tombstone." *Arizona Quarterly Illustrated.* Vol. I, No. 3 (January), p. 22.

_____. 1881. "Election Bulletin—Issued Under the Auspices of the Executive Committee of the Citizens' Protective Party." Tombstone, Arizona, January 4. (This is an election-day handbill promoting John Clum, Ben Sippy, and the other Citizens' Protective Party candidates for Tombstone municipal offices. George Parsons was chairman of the Executive Committee. Photocopy in editor's files.)

_____. 1881. "Citizens' Protective Ticket." *Tombstone Epitaph*, January 4. (The Citizens' Protective Party candidates for the major Tombstone municipal offices were: John P. Clum for mayor; George Pridham, Godfrey Tribolet, Julius A. Kelly, and Smith Gray for councilmen; Ben Sippy for marshal.)

_____. 1881. "The City Election. Overwhelming Success of the Protectives. John P. Clum Elected Mayor of Tombstone. The Townsite Proprietors Get a Black Eye." *Tombstone Epitaph*, January 5 (photocopy in editor's files). (On January 4, 1881, John Clum defeated Mark P. Shaffer in the contest for Tombstone mayor, and Ben Sippy trounced Howard Lee in the race for city marshal. The Citizens' Protective Party candidates for town council seats also were elected.)

_____. 1881. "The many friends of Mayor Clum will sympathize with him in the sorrowful loss he has met with in the death of his infant daughter Bessie, who died in Washington, D.C., on the 7th inst." *Tombstone Daily Nugget*, July 9.

_____. 1881. "Mr. Fred E. Brooks, one of Recorder Jones' efficient deputies, has been promoted by the grace of President Arthur and the United States Senate to the position of postmaster of Tombstone. This is a good appointment, and none of Mr. Brooks friends will congratulate him more heartily upon his political success than the EPITAPH." *Tombstone Epitaph*, December 17.

_____. 1882. "The City Election." *Tombstone Epitaph*, January 4. (On January 3, 1882, John Carr defeated Lewis W. Blinn in the Tombstone mayor's race, and Dave Neagle was elected chief of police, defeating James Flynn and Leslie F. Blackburn.)

_____. 1882. "Pinafore: The rendition of this popular, though much-abused opera, by a company of local amateurs . . . ." *Tombstone Daily Nugget*, May 11.

_____. 1882. "Over the Wires—Capital Notes—Postmaster at Tombstone. The postmaster at Tombstone was settled definitely today by the commissioning of F. E. Brooks as postmaster." *Arizona Daily Star* (Tucson), May 27.

_____. 1882. "John P. Clum is no longer postmaster of Tombstone . . . ." *Tombstone Epitaph*, June 2. (The *Epitaph*, now a Democratic paper, grudgingly acknowledged that Clum had been a very efficient postmaster and criticized the Washington officials who dismissed him.)

_____. 1882. "Cochise County Census." *Tombstone Epitaph*, July 11. (This census counted 9,640 people in the county, 5,300 of them in Tombstone.)

_____. 1885. "The Dramatic Club." *Tombstone Epitaph*, April 10. (Review of the play "The Toodles." Photocopy of article in editor's files.)

_____. 1886. "Esmeralda: An Excellent Dramatic Performance by Our Local Amateurs." *Tombstone Epitaph*, February 19.

Aranda, Daniel D. 1995. "Geronimo's Arrest at Ojo Caliente." *Old West* (Spring), pp. 20-25.

Arizona State Government. 1986. *A Demographic Guide to Arizona.* Population Statistics Unit, Department of Economic Security, Phoenix.

Arizona Territorial Legislature. 1881. "No. 7. An Act to create the County of Cochise . . . . This act shall be in force and take effect from and after its passage. Approved February 1st, 1881." *Acts and Resolutions of the Eleventh Territorial Legislative Assembly of the Territory of Arizona*, pp. 4-7. Office of the Arizona Miner (printer), Prescott.

_____. 1881. "No. 39. An Act to incorporate the City of Tombstone, to define its limits and rights, to specify its privileges and powers and provide for an efficient government for the same . . . . This Act shall take effect and be in force immediately after its passage. Approved February 21st, 1881." *Acts and Resolutions of the Eleventh Legislative Assembly of the Territory of Arizona*, pp. 37-78. Office of the Arizona Miner (printer), Prescott.

Bailey, Lynn R., ed. 1996. *A Tenderfoot in Tombstone: The Private Journal of George Whitwell Parsons—The Turbulent Years, 1880-82.* Westernlore Press, Tucson.

_____. 1997. *The Devil Has Foreclosed: The Private Journal of George Whitwell Parsons, Volume II—The Concluding Arizona Years, 1882-87.* Westernlore Press, Tucson.

Ball, Eve, ed. 1970. *In the Days of Victorio: Recollections of a*

Warm Springs Apache. University of Arizona Press, Tucson.

_____. 1980. *Indeh: An Apache Odyssey.* Reprint: University of Oklahoma Press, Norman, 1988.

Ball, Larry D. 1978. *The United States Marshals of New Mexico and Arizona Territories, 1846-1912.* University of New Mexico Press, Albuquerque.

_____. 1886. "Frontier Sheriffs at Work." *Journal of Arizona History*, Vol. 27, No. 3 (Autumn), pp. 283-296.

_____. 1992. *Desert Lawmen: The High Sheriffs of New Mexico and Arizona, 1846-1912.* University of New Mexico Press, Albuquerque.

Bancroft, Hubert Howe. 1889. *The Works of Hubert Howe Bancroft, Volume XVII: History of Arizona and New Mexico.* The History Company, San Francisco.

Barnes, Will C. 1935. *Arizona Place Names.* Reprint: University of Arizona Press, 1988.

Barrett, S. M., ed. 1906. *Geronimo's Story of His Life.* Reprint: Harlow Publishing Co., Oklahoma City, 1938.

Bell, Bob Boze. 1994. *The Illustrated Life and Times of Doc Holliday.* Tri Star-Boze Publications, Phoenix.

_____. 1995. *The Illustrated Life and Times of Wyatt Earp.* Third edition, revised. Tri Star-Boze Publications, Phoenix.

Berton, Pierre. 1958. *The Klondike Fever: The Life and Death of the Last Great Gold Rush.* Alfred A. Knopf, New York.

Boyer, Glenn G., ed. 1976. *I Married Wyatt Earp: The Recollections of Josephine Sarah Marcus Earp.* University of Arizona Press, Tucson.

Boyer, Glenn G. 1976. "Postscripts to Historical Fiction about Wyatt Earp in Tombstone." *Arizona and the West*, Vol. 18, No. 3 (Autumn), pp. 217-236.

Breakenridge, William M. 1928. *Helldorado: Bringing the Law to the Mesquite.* Reprint: University of Nebraska Press, Lincoln, 1992.

Bret Harte, John. 1972. *The San Carlos Indian Reservation, 1872-1886: An Administrative History.* Two volumes. Unpublished doctoral dissertation, University of Arizona, Tucson.

Brown, Rollin C. "Biographical file." Arizona Historical Society, Tucson. (Includes an unpublished autobiographical memoir.)

Burrows, Jack. 1987. *John Ringo, the Gunfighter Who Never Was.* University of Arizona Press, Tucson.

Butler, Marilyn F., ed. 1996. *Destination Tombstone: Adventures of a Prospector, Edward Schieffelin, Founder of Tombstone, Arizona, 1877.* Royal Spectrum Publishing, Mesa, Arizona.

Byrkit, James W. 1980. "The Word on the Frontier: Anglo Protestant Churches in Arizona, 1859-1899." *Journal of Arizona History*, Vol. 21, No. 1 (Spring), pp. 63-86.

Carmony, Neil B., ed. 1994. *Whiskey, Six-guns & Red-light Ladies: George Hand's Saloon Diary, Tucson, 1875-1878.* High-Lonesome Books, Silver City, New Mexico.

_____. 1995. *How I Routed a Gang of Arizona Outlaws and Other Stories by Wyatt Earp.* Trail to Yesterday Books, Tucson.

_____. 1995. *Next Stop: Tombstone—George Hand's Contention City Diary, 1882.* Trail to Yesterday Books, Tucson.

_____. 1996. *The Civil War in Apacheland: Sergeant George Hand's Diary, California, Arizona, West Texas, New Mexico, 1861-1864.* High-Lonesome Books, Silver City, New Mexico.

Chaput, Don. 1994a. *Virgil Earp, Western Peace Officer.* Reprint: University of Oklahoma Press, Norman, 1996.

Chaput, Don, ed. 1994b. *The Earp Papers: In a Brother's Image.* Affiliated Writers of America, Encampment, Wyoming.

Chaput, Don. 1995. *Nellie Cashman and the North American Mining Frontier.* Westernlore Press, Tucson.

_____. 1996. *Doctor Goodfellow, Physician to the Gunfighters, Scholar and Bon Vivant.* Westernlore Press, Tucson.

Clayton, Wallace E. "Collection." Arizona Historical Society Library, Tucson.

_____. "Collection." Special Collections Department, University of Arizona Library, Tucson.

_____. 1980. "Friend of the Apache, Champion of Tombstone— John Clum." *Tombstone Epitaph* (National Edition), Vol. VII, No. 5 (May), pp. 3-9, 29-31.

_____. 1985. *The Tombstone Epitaph and John Philip Clum.* Red Marie's Bookstore, Tombstone, Arizona.

_____. 1990. "Epitaph Founder Becomes Newsman by Chance." *Tombstone Epitaph* (National Edition), Vol. XVII, No. 5 (May), pp. 7-10, 20.

_____. 1994. "Attempt to Kill Epitaph Editor: Earps, Holliday Also on the Hit List." *Tombstone Epitaph* (National Edition), Vol. CXIV, No. 2 (February), pp. 1, 11.

Clum, Cornelius W. "Biographical records." Montgomery County Historical Society Library, Rockville, Maryland.

Clum, George A. 1929. "Our Advent Into the Great Southwest." *Arizona Historical Review*, Vol. 2, No. 3 (October), pp. 79-87.

Clum, John P. "Biographical file." Alaska State Library, Juneau.

_____. "Collection." Arizona Historical Society Library, Tucson.

_____. "Collection." Special Collections Department, University of Arizona Library, Tucson.

_____. 1880. "The First Trumpet." *Tombstone Epitaph*, May 1. (Clum introduces his newspaper to the Tombstone public. Reprinted in Traywick 1994d, pp. 4-5.)

_____. 1881. "Mayor's Message." *Tombstone Daily Nugget*, January 13. (Reprinted in Traywick 1994d, pp. 28-29.)

_____. 1882. "Our Last Trump." *Tombstone Epitaph*, April 29. (Clum bids farewell to the *Epitaph* but not to Tombstone.)

_____. 1903. "Fighting Geronimo: A Story of the Apache Indian Campaign of 1876." *Sunset*, Vol. XI, No. 1 (May), pp. 36-41.

_____. 1908. "The Clum Record." Fairbanks, Alaska. (Newspaper-like publication promoting Clum's candidacy for delegate to Congress from Alaska.)

_____. 1927. "Santa Fe in the '70s." *New Mexico Historical Review*, Vol. II, No. 4 (October), pp. 380-386.

_____. 1928a. "Geronimo." *New Mexico Historical Review*, Vol. III, No. 1 (January), pp. 1-40; No. 2 (April), pp. 121-144; No. 3 (July), pp. 217-264.

_____. 1928b. "Es-Kim-In-Zin." *New Mexico Historical Review*, Vol. III, No. 4 (October), pp. 399-420; Vol.IV, No. 1 (January 1929), pp. 1-27.

_____. 1929a. "Victorio." *New Mexico Historical Review*, Vol. IV, No. 2 (April), pp. 107-127.

_____. 1929b. "It All Happened in Tombstone." *Arizona Historical Review*, Vol. II, No. 3 (October), pp. 46-72.

_____. 1929c. "The San Carlos Apache Police." *New Mexico Historical Review*, Vol. IV, No. 3 (July), pp. 203-219; Vol. V, No. 1 (January 1930), pp. 1-27.

_____. 1930. "Tombstone's Semi-Centennial." *Arizona Historical Review*, Vol. II, No. 4 (January), pp. 28-30.

_____. 1930. "San Carlos Blasted Into Dust." *Arizona Historical Review*, Vol. III, No. 1 (April), pp. 59-70.

_____. 1930. "Apache Misrule." *New Mexico Historical Review*, Vol. V, No. 2 (April), pp. 138-153; No. 3 (July), pp. 221-239.

_____. 1931. "Apaches as Thespians in 1876." *New Mexico Historical Review*, Vol. VI, No. 1 (January), pp. 76-99.

_____. 1931. "Nellie Cashman." *Arizona Historical Review*, Vol. III, No. 4 (January), pp. 9-34.

_____. 1931. *The Truth About the Apaches Told in the Annual Reports by John P. Clum.* Privately printed in Los Angeles by the author.

_____. 1965. *It All Happened in Tombstone.* Foreword and annotations by John D. Gilchriese. Northland Press, Flagstaff, Arizona. (This slim volume is a reprint of John Clum's 1929 journal article of the same title.)

Clum, John P., as told to J. E. Hogg. 1931. "Apache Years of 'the Man with the High Marble Dome.'" *Touring Topics* (December), pp. 14-17, 45.

Clum, Woodworth. 1936. *Apache Agent: The Story of John P. Clum.* Reprint: University of Nebraska Press, Lincoln, 1978.

_____. N.D. *An Epilogue to Apache Agent.* Privately printed by the author.

Collins, Charles. 1994. *The Great Escape: The Apache Outbreak of 1881.* Westernlore Press, Tucson.

Davis, Britton. 1929. *The Truth About Geronimo.* Reprint: University of Nebraska Press, Lincoln, 1976.

DeArment, Robert K. 1979. *Bat Masterson: The Man and the Legend.* University of Oklahoma Press, Norman.

_____. 1982. *Knights of the Green Cloth: The Saga of the Frontier Gamblers.* University of Oklahoma Press, Norman.

Debo, Angie. 1976. *Geronimo: The Man, His Time, His Place.* University of Oklahoma Press, Norman.

Dunlap, H. E. 1930. "Clay Beauford—Welford C. Bridwell." *Ariz. Historical Review*, Vol. III, No. 3 (October), pp. 44-66.

Erwin, Richard E. 1993. *The Truth About Wyatt Earp.* Second edition. The O.K. Press, Carpintera, California.

Faulk, Odie B. 1972. *Tombstone, Myth and Reality.* Oxford University Press, new York.

Fontana, Bernard L. 1990. "John P. Clum, the Bureaucrat Who Captured Geronimo." *Arizona Highways,* Vol. 66, No. 9 (September), pp. 14-17.

Foster-Harris. 1955. *The Look of the Old West.* Bonanza Books, New York.

Gatto, Steve. 1995. *John Ringo: The Reputation of a Deadly Gunman.* San Simon Publishing, Tucson.

Giese, Dale F. 1991. *Echoes of the Bugle: Forts of New Mexico.* Dale F. Giese, Silver City, New Mexico.

Gilchriese, John D., ed. 1959. "John P. Clum's 'It All Happened In Tombstone.'" *Arizona and the West,* Vol. 1, No. 3 (Autumn), pp. 232-247. (This is an annotated reprint of Clum's 1929 journal article.)

_____. 1975. "Tombstone, Arizona Territory, Circa 1881-82." (Detailed map of downtown Tombstone.)

Gimbert, Sandra L. H. 1988. "1892 Clum House for Sale in Historic District of Kensington, Price is $550,000." *The Journal* (Springfield, Va.), April 22, "Friday Home Report." (This house was built in 1892 and became the home of Cornelius and Mary Clum in 1896.)

Goff, John S. 1978. *Arizona Territorial Officials II: The Governors, 1863-1912.* Black Mountain Press, Cave Creek, Arizona.

_____. 1983. *Arizona Historical Dictionary.* Black Mountain Press, Cave Creek, Arizona.

_____. 1988. *Arizona Territorial Officials IV: The Secretaries, United States Attorneys, Marshals, Surveyors General and*

Superintendents of Indian Affairs, 1863-1912. Black Mountain Press, Cave Creek, Arizona.

_____. 1993. *John C. Fremont.* Arizona Biographical Series. Black Mountain Press, Cave Creek, Arizona.

Granger, Byrd Howell. 1983. *Arizona's Names: X Marks the Place.* Falconer Publishing, Tucson.

Gray, John Pleasant. Ca. 1940. "When All Roads Led to Tombstone." (Unpublished reminiscence in the files of the Arizona Historical Society Library, Tucson.)

Gregory, Leslie E. 1932. "John P. Clum." *Arizona Historical Review*, Vol. V, No. 2 (July), pp. 89-94; No. 3 (October), pp. 188-197.

Hibbs, Jesse (director). 1956. "Walk the Proud Land." (A Hollywood motion picture starring Audie Murphy as Apache Agent John Clum and Jay Silverheels as Geronimo.)

Johnson, David. 1996. *John Ringo.* Barbed Wire Press, Stillwater, Oklahoma.

Jones, A. T. 1882. *Great Register of the County of Cochise, Territory of Arizona, for the Year 1882.* Cochise County Recorder's Office, Tombstone.

_____. 1884. *Great Register of the County of Cochise, Territory of Arizona, for the Year of 1884.* Cochise County Recorder's Office, Tombstone.

_____. 1886. *Great Register of the County of Cochise, Territory of Arizona, for the Year 1886.* Cochise County Recorder's Office, Tombstone.

Keller, Robert H., Jr. 1985. "Shrewd, Able, and Dangerous Men: Presbyterian and Dutch Reformed Indian Agents in the Southwest, 1870-1882." *Journal of Arizona History*, Vol. 26, No. 3 (Autumn), pp. 243-258.

Kelly, George H. 1926. *Legislative History: Arizona, 1864-1912.* Office of the State Historian, Phoenix.

Lake, Carolyn, ed. 1969. *Under Cover for Wells Fargo: The Unvarnished Recollections of Fred Dodge.* Houghton Mifflin, Boston.

Lake, Stuart. 1931. *Wyatt Earp, Frontier Marshal.* Reprint: The Riverside Press, Cambridge, Massachusetts, 1955.

Lamar, Howard R., ed. 1977. *The Reader's Encyclopedia of the American West.* Harper and Row, New York.

Lockley, Fred. N.D. *History of the First Free Delivery Service of Mail in Alaska at Nome, Alaska, in 1900.* Privately published by the author in Portland, Oregon.

Lockwood, Frank C. 1928. "Ed Schieffelin." Reprinted in: *Pioneer Portraits—Selected Vignettes by Frank C. Lockwood,* University of Arizona Press, Tucson, 1968, pp. 179-190.

Lutrell, Estelle. 1949. *Newspapers and Periodicals of Arizona, 1859-1911.* University of Arizona Bulletin No. 15.

Lynch, Sylvia D. 1994. *Aristocracy's Outlaw: The Doc Holliday Story.* Iris Press, New Tazewell, Tennessee.

Lyon, William H. 1994. *Those Old Yellow Dog Days: Frontier Journalism in Arizona, 1859-1912.* Arizona Historical Society, Tucson.

Marcot, Roy M. 1990. *Spencer Repeating Firearms.* R & R Books, Livonia, New York.

Marks, Paula Mitchell. 1989. *And Die in the West: The Story of the O.K. Corral Gunfight.* Reprint: Univ. of Oklahoma Press, Norman, 1996.

Martin, Douglas D., ed. 1951. *Tombstone's Epitaph.* University of New Mexico Press, Albuquerque. (Many early *Epitaph* articles are reprinted in this book.)

_____. 1959. *The Earps of Tombstone.* Tombstone Epitaph, Tombstone, Arizona.

Miller, Nyle H., and Joseph W. Snell, eds. 1963. *Great Gunfighters of the Kansas Cowtowns, 1867-1886.* Reprint: University of Nebraska Press, Lincoln, 1967.

Mulligan, R. A. 1965. *Apache Pass and Old Fort Bowie.* Smoke Signal No. 11. The Tucson Corral of the Westerners.

Myrick, David F. 1967. "The Railroads of Southern Arizona: An Approach to Tombstone." *Journal of Arizona History*, Vol. 8, No. 3 (Autumn), pp. 155-170.

_____. 1975. *Railroads of Arizona, Volume I: The Southern Roads.* Howell-North Books, Berkeley.

Ogle, Ralph H. 1940. *Federal Control of the Western Apaches.* Reprint: University of New Mexico Press, Albuquerque, 1970.

Ortiz, Alfonso, ed. 1983. *Handbook of North American Indians, Volume 10: Southwest.* Smithsonian Institution, Washington, D.C.

Palmquist, Peter E. 1987. "'IT IS AS HOT AS H---.' Carleton E. Watkin's Photographic Excursion Through Southern Arizona, 1880." *Journal of Arizona History*, Vol. 28, No. 4 (Winter), pp. 353-372.

Parker, Marjorie Clum. 1972. "John P. Clum: The Inside Story of an Inimitable Westerner." *The American West*, Vol. 9, No. 1 (January), pp. 32-37.

Parsons, George W. "Diaries." Arizona Historical Society Library, Tucson. (Tombstone pioneer George Parsons kept a daily diary for most of his long life [1850-1933]. The originals covering the period 1879 to 1929 are in the Arizona Historical Society Library in Tucson. Those he kept during his sojourn in Tombstone [1880-1887] were edited by Lynn R. Bailey and published in two volumes—the first appeared in 1996, the other in 1997. In January 1996 the *Tombstone Tumbleweed* newspaper began serializing Parsons' diaries as transcribed by Carl Chafin.)

_____. 1881. "The election of John P. Clum tomorrow is a foregone conclusion with many . . . ." *Tombstone Epitaph*,

January 4. (A plea for John Clum's election as Tombstone mayor.)

Peterson, Thomas H. 1968. *The Tombstone Stagecoach Lines, 1878-1903: A Study in Frontier Transportation*. Unpublished Master of Arts thesis, University of Arizona, Tucson.

Roberts, David. 1993. *Once They Moved Like the Wind: Cochise, Geronimo, and the Apache Wars*. Simon and Schuster, New York.

Rosa, Joseph G. 1993. *Age of the Gunfighter: Men and Weapons on the Frontier, 1840-1900*. Smithmark Publishers, New York.

Ryan, Pat M. 1963. "Sojourn in Santa Fé: John P. Clum's Halcyon Years." *Midwest Review*, Vol. V, pp. 53-61.

_____. 1964. "John P. Clum, Boss-with-the-White-Forehead." *Arizoniana*, Vol. V, No. 3 (Fall), pp. 48-60.

_____. 1965a. "Trail-Blazer of Civilization: John P. Clum's Tucson and Tombstone Years." *Journal of Arizona History*, Vol. VI, No. 2 (Summer), pp. 53-70.

_____. 1965b. "John P. Clum in Alaska." *Alaska Sportsman* (October), pp. 21-23.

_____. 1965c. "Wild Apaches in the Effete East: A Theatrical Adventure of John P. Clum." *Theatre Survey*, Vol. VI, No. 2 (November), pp. 147-156.

_____. 1966. *Tombstone Theatre Tonight! A Chronicle of Entertainment on the Southwestern Mining Frontier*. Smoke Signal No. 13. The Tucson Corral of the Westerners.

Schellie, Don. 1970. *The Tucson* Citizen: *A Century of Arizona Journalism*. Tucson Citizen.

Schieffelin, Edward L. "Collection." Arizona Historical Society Library, Tucson.

Sellers, Frank. 1978. *Sharps Firearms*. Beinfeld Publishing, North Hollywood, California.

Shillingberg, William B. 1976. *Wyatt Earp & the "Buntline Special" Myth.* Blaine Publishing, Tucson.

Sonnichsen, C. L. 1982. *Tucson: The Life and Times of an American City.* University of Oklahoma Press, Norman.

_____. 1986. "From Savage to Saint: A New Image for Geronimo." *Journal of Arizona History*, Vol. 27, No. 1 (Spring), pp. 5-34.

Sorin, Thomas R. 1881. "A Card. Having disposed of my interest in the EPITAPH newspaper, building, etc., to Mr. John P. Clum, I hereby announce my retirement from the firm of Clum, Sorin & Reppy . . . ." *Tombstone (Weekly) Epitaph*, April 11.

Sweeney, Edwin R. 1991. *Cochise, Chiricahua Apache Chief.* University of Oklahoma Press, Norman.

_____. 1992. *Merejildo Grijalva, Apache Captive, Army Scout.* Texas Western Press, El Paso.

Theobald, John, and Lillian Theobald. 1961. *Arizona Territory: Post Offices & Postmasters.* Arizona Historical Foundation, Phoenix.

Thrapp, Dan L. 1967. *The Conquest of Apacheria.* University of Oklahoma Press, Norman.

_____. 1974. *Victorio and the Mimbres Apaches.* University of Oklahoma Press, Norman.

_____. 1988. *Encyclopedia of Frontier Biography.* Three volumes. Reprint: University of Nebraska Press, Lincoln, 1991.

Terrell, John Upton. 1972. *Apache Chronicle.* World Publishing, New York.

Tombstone Common Council. 1880-1887. "Minutes." Copies in the Special Collections Department, University of Arizona Library, Tucson.

Traywick, Ben T., ed. 1988. *History of the Discovery of Tombstone, Arizona, as Told by the Discoverer, Edward Lawrence Schieffelin.* Red Marie's Bookstore, Tombstone, Arizona.

Traywick, Ben T. 1993. *Hell's Belles of Tombstone.* Red Marie's Bookstore, Tombstone, Arizona.

_____. 1994a. *The Chronicles of Tombstone.* Red Marie's Bookstore, Tombstone, Arizona.

_____. 1994b. *Legendary Characters of Southeast Arizona.* Red Marie's Bookstore, Tombstone, Arizona.

_____. 1994c. *Ghost Towns & Lost Treasures.* Red Marie's Bookstore, Tombstone, Arizona.

Traywick, Ben T., ed. 1994d. *Tombstone Clippings.* Red Marie's Bookstore, Tombstone, Arizona.

_____. 1994e. *Historical Documents and Photographs of Tombstone.* Red Marie's Bookstore, Tombstone, Arizona.

Traywick, Ben T. 1996a. *The Clantons of Tombstone.* Red Marie's Bookstore, Tombstone, Arizona.

_____. 1996b. *John Henry (The "Doc" Holliday Story).* Red Marie's Bookstore, Tombstone, Arizona.

Turner, Alford E., ed. 1980. *The Earps Talk.* The early West Series. Creative Publishing, College Station, Texas.

_____. 1981. *The O.K. Corral Inquest.* The Early West Series. Creative Publishing, College Station, Texas.

Underhill, Lonnie E., ed. 1979. "The Tombstone Discovery: The Recollections of Ed Schieffelin & Richard Gird." *Arizona and the West*, Vol. 21, No. 1 (Spring), pp. 37-76.

Van Orden, Jay. 1989. "C. S. Fly at Cañon de los Embudos: American Indians as Enemy in the Field, a Photographic First." *Journal of Arizona History*, Vol. 30, No. 3 (Autumn), pp. 319-346.

Vaughan, Thomas. 1989. "C. S. Fly, Pioneer Photojournalist." *Journal of Arizona History*, Vol. 30, No. 3 (Autumn), pp. 303-318.

Wagoner, Jay J. 1970. *Arizona Territory, 1863-1912: A Political History*. University of Arizona Press, Tucson.

Walker, Henry P. 1969. "Retire Peaceably to Your Homes: Arizona Faces Martial Law, 1882." *Journal of Arizona History*. Vol. 10, No. 1 (Spring), pp. 1-18.

_____. 1974. "Preacher in Helldorado." *Journal of Arizona History*, Vol. 15, No. 3 (Autumn), pp. 223-248.

_____. 1979. "Arizona Land Fraud Model 1880: The Tombstone Townsite Company." *Arizona and the West*, Vol. 21, No. 1 (Spring), pp. 5-36.

Walker, Henry P., and Don Bufkin. 1979. *Historical Atlas of Arizona*. University of Oklahoma Press, Norman.

Walter, Paul A. F. 1932. "John P. Clum." *New Mexico Historical Review*, Vol. VII, No. 3 (July), pp. 292-296.

Washburn, Wilcomb E., ed. 1988. *Handbook of North American Indians, Volume 4: History of Indian-White Relations*. Smithsonian Institution, Washington, D.C.

Waters, Frank. 1960. *The Earp Brothers of Tombstone: The Story of Mrs. Virgil Earp*. Reprint: University of Nebraska Press, Norman, 1976.

INDEX

Agua Prieta, Sonora, 59
Alaska: John Clum in, 74, 84, 88-93; Wyatt Earp in, 74, 91-92
Alaska-Klondike gold rush, 87-91
Albuquerque, 143
Anderson, John J., 159
Antelope Pass, 50, 52
Apache Agent (book), 1
Apache Pass, 102, 105, 111-115, 127, 137
Apaches, Chiricahua. See Chiricahua Apaches
Archer, Robert, 42
Arizona Citizen. See Newspapers
Beauford, Clay (Welford Bridwell), 5, 9, 60, 118-130; photo of, 122
Behan, John, 32-34, 43, 50, 60, 62, 71, 73, 74; photo of, 33
Benson stage, attacks on, 42-44, 68-70
Bilicke, Carl, 71
Bisbee murders and subsequent hangings, 54, 65, 66
Bisbee stage robbery, 47
Blackburn, Leslie F., 75
Blinn, Lewis W., 70
Boot Hill Cemetery, 40
Bowie, Fort. See Military posts
Brady, John, 93
Brazelton, William, 14-17; photo of, 17
Breakenridge, William M. ("Billy"), 47, 50, 96
Bridwell, Welford. See Beauford, Clay

Brocius, "Curly Bill:" shoots Fred White, 44-46; killed by Wyatt Earp, 74
Brooks, Fred Emerson, 39, 67, 70, 77, 80
Brown, Annie, 39
Brown, Rollin C., 13, 23, 25
Brown's Hotel, 75
Bryant, Silas, 50, 162
Campbell & Hatch's Billiard Parlor, 72
Can-Can Restaurant, 59
Captain Jim, 140
Carr, Harry, 95
Carr, John, 70
Casadora, 140; photo of, 153
Cashman, Ellen "Nellie," 64-67, 90, 96; photo of, 90
Centennial Exposition (Philadelphia), 8, 137, 156
Chapin, Dr. S. B., 140, 148
Chapin, Seward B., 159
Charleston, Arizona, 34, 45, 56, 72
Chilkoot Pass (Alaska), 89, 90
Chihuahua, Mexico, 114, 145
Chiricahua Apache Reservation: establishment of, 101, 102; termination of, 6, 7, 104
Chiricahua Apaches: bands of, 6, 7; removal of to San Carlos, 104-118
Citizens' Protective Party, 42, 160
Citizens' Safety Committee, 54
Claiborne, William F. ("Billy"), 59, 61
Clanton, Joseph Isaac ("Ike"), 1, 33, 54-62, 68, 71, 72, 96; photo of, 36

Clanton, Newman H. ("Old Man"), 33, 34; photo of, 35

Clanton, Phineas ("Phin"), 33, 71, 72, 74

Clanton, William H. ("Billy"), 33, 57-61; photo of, 63

Clark, James S., 159

Clum, Belle Atwood (second wife), 80, 81, 93; photo of, 81

Clum, Caro (Caroline, daughter). See Vachon, Caro Clum

Clum, Cornelia (sister), 40

Clum, Cornelius Wilson ("Casey," brother), 39

Clum, Elizabeth ("Bessie," daughter), 40, 46

Clum, Elizabeth Van Deusen (mother), 2, 40

Clum, Florence Baker (third wife), 93, 94

Clum, George Adam (brother), 5

Clum, Jane (sister), 40

Clum, John Philip: early life, 2-4; as Apache agent, 4-10, 101-156; at Florence, 13-17; at Tucson, 18-22; at Tombstone, 23-84; founds and names *Tombstone Epitaph*, 23-29, 37; sells *Tombstone Epitaph*, 74, 75; elected Tombstone mayor, 41, 42; Alaskan adventures, 87-93; last years, 93-97; photos of, op. 1, 3, 7, 19, 28, 81, 91, 92, 95, 103, 108, 153

Clum, Marjorie (granddaughter). See Parker, Marjorie Clum

Clum, Mary Dennison Ware ("Mollie," first wife), 8, 18, 20, 40; photos of, 9, 19

Clum, Mary Greer Herring ("Mamie," Mrs. C. W. Clum), 39

Clum, William Henry (father), 2, 40

Clum, Woodworth (son), 1, 18, 40, 46, 68, 81, 88-91, 157

Coachella Valley, 94

Cochise, 7, 48, 101-104, 108, 118, 145, 151

Cochise County, creation of, 32, 42

Colton, California, 73

Contention City, Arizona, 73, 80; railroad arrives at, 73

Contention Mine, 80

Cosmopolitan Hotel, 71, 75

Crane, Jim, 34, 43

Crook, George, 6, 101

Cruz, Florentino ("Indian Charlie?"), 74

Cunningham, Frances Cashman ("Fanny," Mrs. T. Cunningham), 65

Cunningham, Thomas, 65

Curly Bill. See Brocius, "Curly Bill"

Custer, George, 8, 138, 151

Dake, Crawley, 71, 162

Dawson, Yukon Territory, 90

Dennison, William H., 8

Dexter Saloon (Nome), 91

Diablo, 140; photo of, op. 1

Dodge City, Kansas, 31, 32

Dos Cabezas Mountains, 102, 116, 129

Dragoon Mountains, 40, 49, 50, 70, 74

Dutch Reformed Church, 2-4, 82

Dyea Trail (Alaska), 89
Earp, James, 31, 73
Earp, Josephine (Mrs. Wyatt
    Earp), 94
Earp, Morgan, 31, 43, 47, 50,
    56-63, 72, 73; killed, 72;
    photo of, 58
Earp, Nicholas P., 158
Earp, Virgil, 1, 31, 34, 43, 46,
    47, 50, 56-63, 71-73, 158,
    160, 162; defeated in
    election for Tombstone
    town marshal, 46, 160;
    appointed Tombstone chief
    of police, 46, 47; ambushed
    and disabled, 71; photo of,
    58
Earp, Warren, 31, 72, 74
Earp, Wyatt, 1, 31-34, 43, 45,
    47, 50, 56-63, 71-74, 91,
    94, 157, 158, 162;
    ambiguous politics of, 158;
    photos of, 33, 58, 92
Eccleston, Robert, 41, 42
El Moro, Colorado, 8, 140,
    143, 146, 156
Episcopal Church, 39, 81
Eskiminzin, 1, 48, 140, 146,
    152, 156; photos of, op. 1,
    153
Ewell Springs, 116
Fairbanks, Alaska, 93
Fay, Artemus E., 29
Field, Edward, 159
Fitch, Thomas, 63
Florence, Arizona, 13, 16, 18
Flynn, James, 62, 75
Fly's Photograph Gallery, 60,
    61
Forts and camps. See Military
    posts
Francisco, 125
Frémont, John, 32, 158

French, Charles, 106
Gage, Eliphalet B., 66
Galeyville, Arizona, 45
Galpin, Samuel A., 155
Geronimo, 1, 6, 7, 9, 48-54, 60,
    101-133; photos of, 49, 100
Giddings, Marsh, 3
Gilded Age Mining Claim, 159
Gird, Richard, 29, 34, 96;
    photo of, 30
Globe, Arizona, 20
Goodah-Goodah, 96; photo of,
    96
Goodale, Charles W., 39
Gordo, 125
Grand Central Mill, 70
Grand Central Mine, 66, 80
Grand Hotel, 75
Grant, Ulysses S., 4, 102;
    peace policy of, 4
Gray, Michael, 37
Gray, Smith, 42
Gregory, Carrie, 39
Grijalva, Merejildo
    ("Marijildo"), 105, 140,
    145, 146, 156; photos of,
    108, 141, 153
Gunfight near the O.K. Corral,
    59-61
Hand, George, 73, 107
Hanford, Charlie, 80
Harrington, Jimmie, 68-70
Hartman, Bertha, 39
Harwood, William A., 42
Haslett brothers, 43
Hatch, Bob, 72
Hatch, Edward, 121, 129
Hatton, Frank, 71. 80
Head, Harry, 43
Heath, John, 54, 65; photo of,
    66
Helldorado Days, 94
Henely, Austin, 104, 120

Herring, Mary Greer
("Mamie"). See Clum,
Mary Herring
Herring, William, 39
Hoggatt, Wilford, 93
Holliday, John H. ("Doc"), 32,
43, 59-63, 73, 74, 96; photo
of, 58
Howard, Oliver O., 101, 102,
112, 128, 145, 151
Hoxie, Charles, 91
Huachuca, Camp. See Military
posts
Hugo, William H., 129
Indian Affairs, Office of
(Bureau of Indian Affairs),
Clum hired by, 3, 4
Indian Charlie (Florentino
Cruz?), 72, 74
Ingoldsby, Frank, 50
Jackson, John H., 162
Janos, Chihuahua, 114
Jeffords, Tom, 101, 104, 112,
114; photo of, 113
Johnny-behind-the-deuce, 34,
158
Johnson, Turkey Creek Jack,
74
Joyce, Milt, 32
Juh ("Hoo"), 7, 112, 135
Kautz, August, 5, 104, 105,
107, 109, 112, 120, 135;
photo of, 105
Kelly, Julius A., 42
Killeen, Mike, 157
Kinnear stage, attacks on, 42-
44, 68-70
Klondike-Alaska gold rush, 87-
91
Lackaye, Wilton, 80
Las Palomas, New Mexico,
120, 131
Leatherwood, Robert, 21

Lee, Howard, 42, 46, 160
Leonard, Bill, 43
Leslie, Frank, 157
Levin, Alexander, 20
Linn, Ad, 117
Los Angeles, Clum moves to,
94, 96
McCormick, Richard C., 18
McLaury ("McLowery"),
Frank (Robert F.), 33, 57,
59-61; photos of, 61, 63
McLaury ("McLowery"), Tom,
33, 57, 59-61; photos of, 61,
63
McMasters, Sherman, 74
McNeil, Donald A., 83, 163
McNeil, Bessie (Mrs. D. A.
McNeil), 83. 163
Martin, James P., 107
Military posts (forts and
camps): Apache, 103;
Bayard, 121, 123; Bowie,
102, 104, 111, 114, 115,
120; Grant, 156; Huachuca,
23; Lowell, 14; Union, 123
Miller, John, 16
Mitchell, Alexander J., 39
Morrow, Albert P., 114
Naiche ("Nah-chee"), 48, 103,
109, 112; photos of, 49, 110
Neagle, Dave, 75
Newspapers: *Arizona Citizen*
(Florence), 13, 18; *Arizona
Citizen* (Tucson), 5, 13, 18,
23; *Tombstone Epitaph*,
founding of, 23-29, 37;
Tombstone Epitaph, selling
of, 74, 75; *Tombstone
Nugget*, founding of, 29;
Tombstone Nugget
destroyed by fire, 75
Nolgee, 7, 112
Nome, Alaska, 84, 91

Oakes, James, 111
O'Connor, Dan, 84-86
Ojo Caliente (Warm Springs)
   Reservation, 9, 120-131
O.K. Corral, gunfight near, 59-
   61
Olympic Theatre (St. Louis), 8,
   135, 148-151
Oriental Saloon, 32, 57
O'Rourke, John (Michael?).
   See Johnny-behind-the-
   deuce
Oury, William S., 117
Parker, Marjorie Clum (John
   Clum's granddaughter), 1, 3
Parsons, George W., 40, 42,
   43, 50, 81, 91, 96, 159, 161,
   163; photo of, 41
Paul, Robert, 43; photo of, 44
Philpot, Bud, 43
Pionsenay, 101, 104, 109, 114-
   117, 133
Ponce, 118, 125, 128
Presbyterian Church, 3, 125,
   128
Pridham, George A., 42, 46
Priest, Ward, 50
Purdy, Samuel J., 74, 75
Randall, Alder, 42
Reppy, Charles, 27, 50; picture
   of, 28
Ringo, John, 74
Roerig, Peter, 43
Rogers, Nick, 104, 107, 115
Roosevelt, Theodore, 93
Rouse, John D., 159
Russ House, 64
Rutgers College, 2, 4
Safford, Anson P. K., 115, 118-
   120, 139, 140; photo of,
   119
Sagully, 140; photo of, 153
Samaniego, Mariano, 20

San Bernardino, 84-87
San Carlos Apache
   Reservation, summary of
   Clum's administration of,
   4-10
San Carlos police, 5, 7, 96,
   101-133
San Dimas, California, 94
Sanford, Horatio S., 159
Santa Fe, 2, 3, 121
Schieffelin, Albert, 29, 34, 39,
   96; photo of, 30
Schieffelin, Edward, 23, 29,
   34, 39, 96; photos of, 25, 30
Schieffelin Hall, 39, 67, 82
Schneider, W. P., killing of, 34
Sergeant Rip, 125, 128
Shaffer, Mark P., 41, 42
Shibell, Charles, 32, 117, 133,
   158; photo of, 132
Short, Luke, 32
Sieber, Al, 23
Signal Service, U.S. Army, 2, 3
Silver City, 121, 128-131, 142,
   143
Sippy, Ben, 34, 42, 46, 47, 160;
   defeats Virgil Earp in
   election for Tombstone
   town marshal, 46; defeats
   Howard Lee in election for
   Tombstone town marshal,
   42, 160
Skinya ("Skin-yea"), 103, 104,
   108, 109
Smallpox, 130, 131
Smith, John Quincy, 104, 121,
   151, 154
Sneezer, 96; photo of, 96
Sorin, Thomas, 27; picture of,
   28
Southern Pacific Railroad, 18,
   43, 93 94
Spence, O. O., 104, 107, 115

Spence (Spencer?), Pete, 47, 72, 74, 160
Spicer, Wells, 57, 62, 63
Stilwell, Frank, 47, 72, 73
Stilwell, William H., 72
Storms, Charlie, 32
Sulphur Springs Stage Station, 104, 109, 111
Sulphur Springs Valley, 49, 50, 59, 109, 116
Summers, H. B., 13
Sweeney, Martin A., 5, 130
Taza ("Tah-zay"), 7, 8, 101, 103, 104, 109, 112, 114, 140, 145, 146, 151, 152; photo of, 152
Telephone (in Tombstone), 70
Toland, Clarence G., 95
Tombstone: founding of, 23, 37, 42; incorporation of, 42, 46; population of, 29, 94; fires in, 46, 75; decline of, 80
Tombstone Amateur Dramatic Club, 39, 82, 83
Tombstone Epitaph. See Newspapers
Tombstone Nugget. See Newspapers
Tombstone Townsite Company, 37, 159
Tribolet, Godfrey, 42
Tucson: George Clum moves to, 5; John Clum's life in, 13, 18-22; Apache police hold pow-pow in, 105-107; Apache militia delivered to Governor Safford at, 119, 120
Turn Verein Hall, 75
Vachon, Caro Clum (Mrs. P. A. Vachon), 80, 81, 93; photo of, 81

Vachon, Peter A., 93
Vermillion, Texas Jack, 74
Victorio, 9, 120, 129, 135
Wade, James F., 123, 128
Wallace, Albert O., 56
Ward, Jerome, 66
Ware, Mary Angelina (Mrs. T. D. Ware, J. P. Clum's mother-in-law), 40, 46
Ware, Mary Dennison. See Clum, Mary Ware
Ware, Thomas D., 8
Warm Springs Reservation. See Ojo Caliente
Wasson, John, 13, 18, 26
Whistling Dick. See Wright, Dick
White, Fred, 44-46
Wickersham, James, 93
Williams, Marshall, 47, 50, 63
Williams, Tom, 117
Williams, Wheeler W., 20
Willis, George C., 39
Wilson, Ed, 84
Woods, Henry M. ("Harry"), 158
Wright, Dick ("Whistling Dick"), 69
Yukon Territory, 87-90